STATE OF NITA

V.

DANNY DAWSON

SECOND EDITION

STATE OF NITA

V.

DANNY DAWSON

SECOND EDITION

American Mock Trial Association

NITA®

NATIONAL INSTITUTE FOR TRIAL ADVOCACY

Address inquiries to:

Reprint Permission
National Institute for Trial Advocacy
1685 38th Street, Suite 200
Boulder, CO 80301-2735
Phone: (800) 225-6482
Fax: (720) 890-7069
E-mail: permissions@nita.org

ISBN 978-1-60156-551-8 (print)
eISBN 978-1-60156-552-5 (eBook)
FBA 1551

Printed in the United States of America

 Wolters Kluwer

Official co-publisher of NITA.
WKLegaledu.com/NITA

Acknowledgments

The AMTA Criminal Case Committee would like to thank:

- **The American Law Institute**, whose Model Penal Code continues to serve legal education.

- **Chris Hutchison**, Assistant Commonwealth's Attorney (Louisville, KY) and Division Chief of his office's F.A.S.T. Team, which is responsible for the prosecution of individuals involved in motor-vehicle collisions in which someone has been killed, injured, or endangered.

- **Roman Kickirillo**, professional accident reconstruction expert for Kickirillo Engineering PLLC (Nashville, TN), and **Sergeant Andy Shelton** of the Tennessee State Highway Patrol.

- **Chatterbox Audio Theater** (Memphis, TN) for its assistance in recording AMTA's first audio exhibit. http://www.chatterboxtheater.org/

- **Carly Taylor** and **Chris Guyot** for providing background music for the audio recording. Their song, "Love the Sinner, Hate the Sin," may be heard in its entirety at http://soundcloud.com/taylorcarlyj/love-the-sinner-hate-the-sin/

Disclaimer

CASE SUMMARY

On September 24, YR-2, Vanessa Sullivan, daughter of Nita's most prominent prosecutor, celebrated her twenty-first birthday with two friends, Taylor Hopson and Danny Dawson, at Chuggie's Sports Bar. After several hours of celebration at the bar, the three left in a car driven by Dawson. On the way home Dawson lost control of the car, resulting in a crash in which Sullivan was killed.

A special prosecutor was appointed because of the conflict of interest in having the victim's parent's office prosecute the case. A grand jury has returned a multi-count indictment charging the defendant, Danny Dawson, with murder and driving under the influence.

ELECTRONIC EXHIBITS

Electronic versions of the exhibits are available for download here http://bit.ly/1P20Jea

Password: Dawson1

CONTENTS

AFFIDAVITS

SPECIAL INSTRUCTIONS

1. Witness Availability.

   a. The following witness must be called by the prosecution: **Avery Smith**, Director, Nita Department of Forensics.

   b. The following witnesses are available only to the prosecution: **Taylor Hopson**, best friend of victim; **Ryan Foster**, police officer; **Pat Lawrence**, server at Chuggie's.

   c. The following witnesses are available only to the defense: **Leslie Roman**, accident reconstruction expert; **Danny Dawson**, defendant; **Ashley Norton**, medical expert; **Jordan James**, musician and bartender at Chuggie's.

   d. The following witnesses are available either to the prosecution or defense: **Sam Lyons**, cab driver; **London Bennett**, eyewitness at the scene; **Sandy Cullen**, eyewitness at police station.

2. Witness Call Order.

   The prosecution must first announce whether it will call Ryan Foster.

   If:

   a. the prosecution elects to call Avery Smith *and* Ryan Foster,

      i. the defense must next call either Ashley Norton or Leslie Roman;

      ii. The remaining witnesses are selected in the following order: **D-D-P** (note that the defense may choose to call both Norton and Roman by using one of their final two calls to select the defense expert not selected earlier);

   b. the prosecution elects to call Avery Smith, but *not* Ryan Foster,

      i. the defense *must* call Ashley Norton;

      ii. the next witnesses are selected in the following order: **P-D-D-P**; if—and only if—the defense chooses Leslie Roman with any of its picks, the prosecution may respond (if it so chooses) by calling Ryan Foster with its final pick.

3. Witnesses Not Present.

   a. If the defense has not called Danny Dawson and will not have Dawson present in the courtroom, the defense must notify the prosecution whether Danny Dawson is male or female.

b. Then if the prosecution does not call Taylor Hopson, the prosecution must notify the defense whether Taylor Hopson is male or female.

4. Indictment / Lesser Included Offenses.

   a. The charging instrument (often called the "grand jury indictment" or "trial information") in most jurisdictions does not contain what are commonly referred to as "lesser included offenses." Lesser included offenses are less severe conviction options that could be supported by the facts once all evidence has been entered. They are often sought by the defense for strategic reasons at the close of proof, prior to closing arguments. Since attorneys in Nita may not argue for particular jury instructions, all potential lesser included criminal-homicide offenses have been incorporated into the Indictment, Jury Instructions, and Verdict Forms.

   b. The prosecution *must* pursue the top count of Murder and the single count of DUI.

   c. The defense is free to argue for the defendant's being not guilty on all criminal-homicide charges (murder, manslaughter, and reckless homicide) or for the defendant's being not guilty of the top criminal-homicide charge, but perhaps guilty of one or more of the lesser included criminal-homicide offenses.

   [handwritten note in left margin: can argue guilty of a lesser included offense]

   d. The defense is *not* permitted to concede the DUI charge prior to closing argument, but need not address it directly in its opening statement or case-in-chief. Thus, in an objection argument, the defense cannot claim that a certain element of the prosecution's case is irrelevant because the defense is not contesting the DUI charge.

5. General Rules Regarding Case Materials.

   a. No witness may deny the authenticity of a document or exhibit in the case packet, although if a witness is not familiar with the document in question, that witness may testify to that fact.

   b. A witness whose affidavit or report states that the witness is familiar with a particular document or exhibit must acknowledge, if asked, that he or she is familiar with that document or exhibit and that the document or exhibit referenced in the affidavit or report is the same version as the corresponding document in the current case materials. This does not relieve the party offering the document or exhibit of its obligation to provide sufficient foundation to establish admissibility.

   c. The only judicial decisions that may be referenced are those included in the case packet. The portions of the Nita statutes provided under "Nita Penal Code" represent all of the relevant statutes for this case.

   d. The parties have raised all objections arising under the United States Constitution prior to trial in motions in limine and preserved them for appeal. Accordingly, no party may raise any objections specifically related to the United States Constitution at trial. All such objections have previously been overruled, and no motion for reconsideration is permitted.

6. Audio Exhibit.

An audio file (downloadable by both Macs and PCs) is available as an exhibit in this case. The audio file exhibit is subject to objections under the rules of evidence, statutes, and case law. If it is admitted during trial, then the audio file exhibit is subject to the following rules on how it may be published:

a. The *only* audio recording that may be introduced at trial is Exhibit 1(a), the voicemail recording available for download at http://bit.ly/1P20Jea (Password: Dawson1).

a. Exhibit 1(b) is the transcript of that audio recording. The transcript may be provided to judges/jurors to read along with the recording while it is being played, but the transcript itself may not be entered into evidence.

7. Photograph of Vanessa Sullivan.

a. The prosecution may provide a photograph of the deceased victim, Vanessa Sullivan.

b. The photograph may not contain any other person in addition to Vanessa Sullivan or anything specifically intended to evoke other persons, places, things, or events specifically mentioned or described in the case (e.g., "Chuggie's" front window, "Chatterbox" t-shirt, sign saying "Danny is My Designated Driver," etc.).

c. The person portraying Vanessa Sullivan in the photograph must appear to be reasonably close to Vanessa Sullivan's age shortly before her death (i.e., twenty years old) and must not show any signs of death or injury (i.e., these are not post-crash photographs).

d. At trial, the defense may not raise objections based on the restrictions listed herein, but may still raise objections based on the Nita Rules of Evidence.

8. Jury Instructions/Verdict Forms.

a. *Origin of Jury Instructions/Verdict Forms.* It is presumed that the Jury Instructions/Verdict Forms included in the case packet are the product of the typical court and counsel interplay (often referred to as charging hearings) and that any objections to their final form have been preserved. No changes to the provided Jury Instructions/Verdict Forms may be sought or made.

b. *Use of Jury Instructions/Verdict Forms.* For purposes of this trial, the judge will be presumed to have read the Jury Instructions/Verdict Forms included in the case packet to the jury after both sides have concluded their cases-in-chief and before either side presents its closing argument.

c. *Before closing arguments.* At any time before closing arguments, attorneys may reference case law and statutory law (e.g., in objection arguments). Attorneys may not reference the Jury Instructions/Verdict Forms before closing arguments.

d. *During closing arguments.* When referring to matters of law during closing arguments, attorneys should reference the law as set forth in the Jury Instructions/Verdict Forms, not the case law or statutory law in the case packet.

e. *Providing copies of Jury Instructions/Verdict Forms.* Either party (or both) may, but is not required to, provide complete, unedited copies of the Jury Instructions/Verdict Forms to the judges/jurors prior to closing arguments, and no objection to their being given to judges/jurors may be raised (except, of course, if the jury instructions/verdict forms being offered are not a complete and accurate copy of the Jury Instructions/Verdict Forms included in the case packet). Teams are encouraged to consult with practitioners regarding appropriate and effective use of jury instructions during closing arguments.

f. *Use of Defendant's Affidavit during trial.* In an actual criminal trial, a defendant cannot be compelled to provide an affidavit because of the Fifth Amendment provision regarding self-incrimination. In mock trial, such an affidavit is necessary to define and confine the defendant's testimony and knowledge. Thus, the defendant's affidavit cannot be referenced during the testimony of a witness other than the defendant nor at any other time during either party's case-in-chief, except during direct or cross-examination of the defendant. Use of the defendant's affidavit during direct and cross-examination of the defendant is subject to the Nita Rules of Evidence. This rule does not prohibit reference during closing arguments to any impeachment of the defendant.

9. *Kane Software Co. v. Mars Investigations*, included in the Available Case Law, does not create any new obligation or requirement. All information disclosed in the expert's affidavit, report, and any other documents with which the witness is familiar is presumed to have been provided to both parties. Thus, for the purpose of satisfying the requirements of *Kane*:

    a. no additional disclosure of the expert's conclusions, facts, etc., is *necessary*; and

    b. no disclosure of additional facts or conclusions of an expert beyond the case materials is *permitted.*

IN THE CIRCUIT COURT OF DARROW COUNTY, NITA

CRIMINAL COURT DIVISION

STATE OF NITA,

    Plaintiff,

v.   CASE NO. CR-YR-1-1030

DANNY DAWSON,

    Defendant.

INDICTMENT

THE GRAND JURY DOES HEREBY CHARGE:

COUNT I: On or about September 25, YR-2, in Darrow County, State of Nita, Danny Dawson did extremely recklessly kill Vanessa Sullivan, a human being, by injuring her in a motor vehicle crash in violation of N.P.C. 210.2.

COUNT II: On or about September 25, YR-2, in Darrow County, State of Nita, Danny Dawson did recklessly kill Vanessa Sullivan, a human being, by injuring her in a motor vehicle crash in violation of N.P.C. 210.3.

COUNT III: On or about September 25, YR-2, in Darrow County, State of Nita, Danny Dawson did negligently kill Vanessa Sullivan, a human being, by injuring her in a motor vehicle crash in violation of N.P.C. 210.4.

COUNT IV: On or about September 25, YR-2, in Darrow County, State of Nita, Danny Dawson did operate a motor vehicle under the influence of alcohol in violation of N.P.C. 510.1.

A TRUE BILL OF INDICTMENT

October 27, YR-2 _____   _____/S/_____

Dated   Foreperson of the Grand Jury,

                                            Darrow County, Nita

Nita Penal Code

(Selected Provisions)

PART I. GENERAL PROVISIONS

Article 1. Preliminary [Omitted]

Article 2. General Principles of Liability

SECTION 2.01. [Omitted]

SECTION 2.02. General Requirements of Culpability.

(1) **Minimum Requirements of Culpability.** A person is not guilty of an offense unless he acted purposefully, knowingly, recklessly, or negligently, as the law may require, with respect to each material element of the offense.

(2) **Kinds of Culpability Defined.**

    (a) *Purposefully.* A person acts purposefully with respect to a material element of an offense when:

        (i) if the element involves the nature of his conduct or a result thereof, it is his conscious objective to engage in conduct of that nature or to cause such a result; and

        (ii) if the element involves the attendant circumstances, he is aware of the existence of such circumstances or he believes or hopes they exist.

    (b) *Knowingly.* A person acts knowingly with respect to a material element of an offense when:

        (i) if the element involves the nature of his conduct or the attendant circumstances, he is aware that his conduct is of that nature or that such circumstances exist; and

        (ii) if the element involves a result of his conduct, he is aware that it is practically certain that his conduct will cause such a result.

    (c) *Recklessly.* A person acts recklessly with respect to a material element of an offense when he consciously disregards a substantial and unjustifiable risk that the material element exists or will result from his conduct. The risk must be of such a nature and degree that considering the nature and purpose of the actor's conduct and the circumstances known to him, its disregard involves a gross deviation from the standard of conduct that a law-abiding person would observe in the actor's situation.

    (d) *Negligently.* A person acts negligently with respect to a material element of an offense when he should be aware of a substantial and unjustifiable risk that the material element exists or will result from his conduct. The risk must be of such a nature and degree that the actor's failure to perceive it, considering the nature and purpose of his conduct and the circumstances known to him, involves a gross deviation from the standard of care that a reasonable person would observe in the actor's situation.

PART II. DEFINITION OF SPECIFIC CRIMES

OFFENSES INVOLVING DANGER TO THE PERSON

Article 210. Criminal Homicide

SECTION 210.1. Criminal Homicide

(1) A person is guilty of criminal homicide if he purposefully, knowingly, recklessly, or negligently causes the death of another human being.

(2) Criminal homicide is murder, manslaughter, or negligent homicide.

SECTION 210.2. Murder

(1) Except as provided in Section 210.3(1)(b), criminal homicide constitutes murder when:

    (a) it is committed purposely or knowingly; or

    (b) it is committed recklessly under circumstances manifesting extreme indifference to the value of human life.

(2) Murder is a felony in the first degree.

SECTION 210.3. Manslaughter

(1) Criminal homicide constitutes manslaughter when:

    (a) it is committed recklessly; or

    (b) [OMITTED].

(2) Manslaughter is a felony of the second degree.

SECTION 210.4. Negligent Homicide

(1) Criminal homicide constitutes negligent homicide when it is committed negligently.

(2) Negligent homicide is a felony of the third degree.

* * *

SECTION 510.1. Driving Under the Influence.

(1) A person shall not operate or be in physical control of a motor vehicle anywhere in this state:

    (a) Having an alcohol concentration of 0.08 or more as measured by a scientifically reliable test or tests of a sample of the person's breath or blood taken within two (2) hours of cessation of operation or physical control of a motor vehicle; or

must be breath/blood w/in 2 hours of driving

    (b) While under the influence of alcohol.

(2) Driving under the influence is a misdemeanor of the first degree.

AVAILABLE CASE LAW

Criminal Homicide

State v. Jeffries (YR-40)

In a murder case, a defendant may be found guilty of murder in the absence of a specific intent to kill where an act was done with such heedless disregard of a harmful result, foreseen as a likely possibility, that it differs little in the scale of moral blameworthiness from an actual intent to cause such harm. To distinguish such a crime from "intentional murder," it is useful to call it "extreme reckless murder" and to distinguish its mens rea from specific intent to kill by calling it "constructive malice." *this is count one*

State v. Maddox (YR-38)

A trial court may not prevent a case of murder from going to the jury under an "extreme reckless murder" theory if the evidence, viewed as a whole, could be reasonably interpreted as showing the type of heightened recklessness that equates to purposeful or knowing homicide. *heightened recklessness that equates to purposeful or knowing homicide*

State v. Borris (YR-17)

The fact that a motorist was operating a vehicle under influence of intoxicants at the time of an accident does not, in and of itself, suffice to establish extreme recklessness under the Nita Penal Code. *fact drunk when driving does NOT itself est. extreme recklessness*

State v. Harding (YR-13)

The Nita Supreme Court upheld a conviction for reckless murder in a vehicular-homicide case, holding that "the facts show[ed] a deviation from established standards of regard for life and the safety of others markedly different in degree from the negligence found in most vehicular homicides." *↳ successful vehic. homicide case proved these things*

Burden of Proof

State v. Monarch (YR-108)

In a criminal case, the burden of proof is on the State and never shifts to the defendant. The standard of proof in a criminal case is beyond a reasonable doubt with respect to each and every element of the offense(s) alleged.

State v. Sarobe (YR-31)

The State's burden of proving its case beyond a reasonable doubt applies to each and every element of the crime charged, but this burden does not operate on the many subordinate, evidentiary, or incidental facts as distinguished from proof of the elements of the crime or of an ultimate fact. Where, however, the State relies in whole or in part on circumstantial evidence to prove an element of a crime, although each link in the chain of evidence to support it need not be proven beyond a reasonable doubt, the cumulative impact of that evidence must, in order to support that inference, convince the finder of fact beyond a reasonable doubt that the element has been proven.

Richey v. Bartlett (YR-10)

In all trials, fact finders may rely on both direct and circumstantial evidence. Direct evidence is testimony by a witness about what that witness personally did, saw, or heard. Circumstantial evidence is indirect evidence from which the fact finder may infer that another fact is true. Physical evidence may fall into either category. Neither type of evidence should be given categorically more weight than the other.

State v. Tamase (YR-40)

It is up to the fact finder to determine the credibility of each witness's testimony. A fact finder, whether jury or judge, may choose to credit all, some, or none of a witness's testimony. At all times, the fact finder may consider the witness's interest in the outcome of the case.

State v. Lowe (YR-27)

A criminal defendant's decision to exercise the constitutionally protected right not to testify in his or her own defense may not be commented upon by either party, either explicitly or implicitly. However, if the defendant does choose to testify, his or her credibility is to be judged like that of any other witness.

Expert Testimony

Davis v. Adams (YR-19)

Under the Nita Rules of Evidence, trial judges must ensure that any and all scientific testimony or evidence admitted is not only relevant, but reliable. In determining whether expert testimony is sufficiently reliable to be admitted, judges should consider only the methods employed and the data relied upon, not the conclusions themselves.

Tarot Readers Association of Nita v. Merrell Dow (YR-18)

In assessing reliability under *Davis v. Adams*, judges should consider, among other factors, whether the theory or technique has been or can be tested, whether it has been subjected to peer review and publication, whether it has a known error rate, and whether it has gained widespread acceptance within the field. These factors, while relevant, are not necessarily dispositive. For example, lack of publication does not automatically foreclose admission; sometimes well-grounded, but innovative theories will not have been published. Indeed, there is no definitive checklist in making a preliminary assessment of whether reasoning or methodology underlying expert testimony is scientifically reliable. Judges must make such assessments based on the totality of the circumstances, and the proponent of such expert testimony must meet the threshold proof requirement of a preponderance of the evidence.

Kane Software Co. v. Mars Investigations (YR-17)

Prior to trial, the party offering an expert must provide the identity of the expert, identify the sources of information underlying the expert's conclusions (including but not limited to affidavits, depositions, and/or written reports), state the basis of the expert's conclusions and the conclusions themselves, and identify all relevant expertise that qualifies the witness to testify to such conclusions. If such disclosure to opposing counsel is not made prior to trial or if the expert's testimony at trial is so materially different from that disclosed prior to trial that admitting it would result in unfair surprise or trial by ambush, the court may exclude the offending portion(s) of the expert's testimony at trial.

Richards v. Mississippi BBQ (YR-15)

Nita Rule of Evidence 703 does not afford an expert unlimited license to testify or present a chart in a manner that simply summarizes the testimony of others without first relating that testimony to some "specialized knowledge" on the expert's part as required under Nita Rule of Evidence 702. The court must distinguish experts relying on hearsay to form scientific conclusions from conduits who merely repeat what they are told. The testimony of the former is admissible; that of the latter is not.

Breath Alcohol and Field Sobriety Tests

State v. Harper (YR-17)

Although the Court is aware that the states are split on the issue, the Nita Supreme Court unanimously holds that a law enforcement officer can lawfully compel an individual suspected of a DUI offense to perform a field sobriety test and/or a breath alcohol test. If the accused refuses, the State can elicit testimony regarding the individual's refusal as evidence of a person's consciousness of guilt. Like many of our sister states taking this position, we hold that the law-enforcement officer does not have to inform the accused that this refusal may be held against her.

Other Evidentiary Issues

State v. Chenault (YR-22)

In a criminal case, a police officer is not considered a "party opponent" for the purpose of admissibility of a statement made by that officer under Nita Rule of Evidence 801(d)(2). This does not preclude the admissibility of the officer's statement under other applicable provisions of the Nita Rules of Evidence.

State v. Spears (YR-20)

[handwritten annotation: limits admissibility of statements by prosecutors not involved in case from being opposing party stmts.]

In a criminal case, the defendant sought introduction of a statement made by an Assistant District Attorney to an officer involved in the investigation of the crime at issue. The statement was made prior to the filing of an indictment, and the Assistant District Attorney was no longer employed by the State at the time of indictment. The State objected to admission of the statement as hearsay, and the trial court overruled the objection, admitting the statement as an admission by a party opponent under Nita Rule of Evidence 801(d)(2). On interlocutory appeal, the Nita Court of Appeals overturned the ruling, expanding its prior ruling in *State v. Chenault* to encompass statements by any state official not currently involved in the prosecution of the criminal matter at trial. Finding insufficient evidence in the record to consider other grounds for admissibility, the Nita Court of Appeals instructed the trial court to consider whether the statement was admissible under any other provision or theory under the Nita Rules of Evidence.

IN THE CIRCUIT COURT OF DARROW COUNTY, NITA

CRIMINAL COURT DIVISION

STATE OF NITA,

    Plaintiff,

v.

CASE NO. CR-YR-1-1030

DANNY DAWSON,

    Defendant.

ORDER ON MOTIONS IN LIMINE

This matter came to be heard on the 15th day of August, YR-1, upon pretrial motions by counsel in the above-referenced case. Upon review of the facts and the arguments of counsel, the Court finds and orders as follows:

A.   <u>Defendant's Motion for Change of Venue or, alternatively, to Appoint Special Counsel.</u>

1. All of the alleged conduct listed in the State's indictment occurred within Darrow County and venue in this jurisdiction is proper.

2. The alleged victim in this case is a close relative of the District Attorney for the county of jurisdiction in this offense, District Attorney Ryan Sullivan.

3. In considering a Motion for Change of Venue, the Court is compelled to balance the factors of convenience of the parties and witnesses and the interest of justice, which includes a consideration of 1) the location of the Defendant, 2) the location of possible witnesses, 3) the location of events likely to be in issue, 4) the location of documents and records likely to be involved, 5) disruption of Defendant's business unless the case is transferred, 6) the docket of each district and division involved, 7) the location of counsel, 8) relative accessibility of the place of trial, 9) expense to the parties, and 10) any other special elements that may affect the transfer.

4. This Court is persuaded by arguments from the Government that these factors on balance weigh in favor of retaining venue in Nita Center, Darrow County. The only persuasive argument by the Defense for moving this case is that the victim, Vanessa Sullivan, was the only

daughter of District Attorney Ryan Sullivan. Defendant's argument that Defendant resides in another city is not persuasive in light of Court's conclusion that the other witnesses, documents, and surrounding events are located in or related to this venue. This Court does, however, find that Defendant is entitled to the appointment of Special Prosecution Counsel from outside the office of District Attorney Sullivan. Therefore, Defendant's *Motion for Change of Venue* is hereby **DENIED** and the alternative *Motion by Defendant to Appoint Special Counsel* is hereby **GRANTED**.

WHEREFORE, this Court holds that upon the entry of this order, Special Counsel from Polk County shall be appointed for the purpose of representing the State of Nita in the pursuit of justice in the foregoing matter.

B.   State's Motion to Admit Audio Recordings.

1.   State's counsel issued a subpoena to Nita Global Knowledge Wireless ("NGK Wireless"), a wireless telecommunication provider, on October 12, YR-2. The subpoena ordered the production of all information, text messages, voicemails, and data transmitted to and from NGK Wireless telephone number 555-272-7376, which was registered to Vanessa Sullivan, an NGK Wireless subscriber, sent or received from 1800 on September 24, YR-2, through 0200 on September 25, YR-2.

2.   NGK Wireless timely responded to the subpoena, and copies of all materials produced pursuant to the subpoena were produced upon a Motion for Discovery by the Defense.

3.   Among the data received from NGK Wireless was a voicemail recording from 555-272-7376 to phone number 555-715-5507 at 12:57 a.m. on September 25, YR-2.

4.   Upon the sworn declaration of Olivia Wolbert, employee and record keeper with NGK Wireless, this Court is satisfied that number 555-715-5507 belongs to Francis Sullivan, parent of Vanessa Sullivan and spouse of Ryan Sullivan. This was confirmed in a sworn affidavit provided by Ryan Sullivan, who shares a family account plan with Vanessa Sullivan and Francis Sullivan.

5.   State's counsel moved in limine to admit the audio recordings for use at trial.

6.   Defendant has raised several objections to the introduction of this evidence by the Government at trial, including lack of authentication, hearsay, and danger of unfair prejudice. Upon consideration of these objections by the Defense, this Court finds as follows:

    a.   The statements contained in above paragraphs (B)(1) through (B)(4) shall be taken as findings of fact.

    b.   Defendant's objections to lack of authentication, hearsay, and danger of unfair prejudice are best handled at trial. Although the findings of fact in paragraphs (B)(1) through (B)(4) have some bearing on those evidentiary arguments, the trial court will be in the best position to adjudicate this matter.

WHEREFORE, State's Motion to Admit the Audio Recording is hereby **RESERVED**, subject to the following limitations:

a. If the audio file is admitted at trial, upon its first publication, the audio file must be played/published in its entirety before the jury. Thereafter, should the audio be used subsequently through witnesses or in closing arguments, the audio file may be stopped/started and need not be played in its entirety.

b. If the audio file is admitted at trial, a transcript of the audio may be provided to the judge and parties during the trial, but may not be admitted as an exhibit.

C.   Defendant's Motion to Exclude Character Evidence under Rules 404 and 608–609.

Defendant has reserved the right to object to any evidence put forth by the Government regarding the past consumption of alcohol by the Defendant, past instances of driving under the influence or driving recklessly, or any other past conduct put forth in an effort by the Government to show action in conformity therewith. The Government responded that any attempts to use such evidence would be permissible under the exceptions to Rule 404(b) to the extent such use would demonstrate knowledge, intent, or lack of mistake. The Government additionally requested notice from the Defense of any character evidence of the accused that the Defense intended to offer under N.R.E. 404(a). Defendant objects to the Government's request.

The jurisdiction of Nita is unique in that it prohibits the Government from calling rebuttal witnesses. Normally, the Government's use of specific instances of conduct in the manner proscribed by the State would be appropriate in rebuttal form once the Defendant has alleged counter-evidence in the form of mistake, lack of knowledge, or lack of intent. Similarly, the Government would be able to recall witnesses to respond to any attempts by the Defendant to demonstrate general traits for carefulness, nonrecklessness, or other traits relevant to the charges. However, since there are no rebuttal witnesses, for the purpose of this trial, the Court orders as follows:

1. The Defense must provide the Government with notice of any intent by the Defense to offer evidence of the character of the Defendant related to the Defendant's general character for carefulness, safety, or other relevant traits related to the charges. This notice must be provided prior to the start of trial and must be signed by lead counsel for each party.

2. The Government must offer similar notice to the Defense regarding its intent to use specific instances of conduct for knowledge, lack of mistake, intent, or any other permissible reason set forth in 404(b).

3. Upon receipt of notice by Defendant that the Defense intends to offer evidence under 404(a), the Government may pursue "preemptory rebuttal evidence" of competing traits during its case-in-chief. If the Defendant does not provide notice of its intent to offer 404(a) evidence, neither party may introduce such evidence at trial.

The Defendant also objects to the introduction of any character evidence offered by the Government pursuant to N.R.E. 608 and 609. Since N.R.E. 608 and 609 only apply to testifying witnesses, this

Court has reserved ruling on these objections as they apply to the Defendant, or any other witness, until trial, but does require both parties to comply with the same notice requirements set forth in the paragraphs relating to evidence submitted under N.R.E. 404.

IT IS HEREBY ORDERED, ADJUDGED, AND DECREED.

_____/s/_____
Hon. Alfred Wayne
State of Nita
August 16, YR-1

IN THE CIRCUIT COURT OF DARROW COUNTY, NITA

CRIMINAL COURT DIVISION

STATE OF NITA,

    Plaintiff,

v.

                                                    CASE NO. CR-YR-1-1030

DANNY DAWSON,

    Defendant.

STIPULATIONS

1. The parties agree that the transcript of the audio recording, Exhibit 1(b), is authentic, accurate, and complete for the purpose of its being provided to judges/jurors to follow along with the audio recording itself, Exhibit 1(a), when the audio recording is published to the jury at trial. All objections to either party providing the transcript to the judges/jurors for that limited purpose, and only for that limited purpose, are waived. The parties agree that the transcript will not be entered into evidence.

2. The signatures on the receipts from Chuggie's Sports Bar—Exhibits 2(a), 2(b), and 2(c)— are in fact those of the indicated individuals (Danny Dawson, Danny Dawson, and Vanessa Sullivan, respectively). Both parties have waived any and all objections as to the authenticity of those signatures.

3. A single-car collision that occurred at approximately 1:00 a.m. on the morning of September 25, YR-2, was the sole cause of the death of Vanessa Sullivan. Danny Dawson was the driver of the car at the time of the collision.

4. All photographs in Exhibit 13 are unaltered and represent what they purport to represent. The parties hereby stipulate that the car in accident photos 0001–0009 is the YR-3 Chevrolet Impala driven by the defendant, Danny Dawson, on September 25, YR-2. The parties agree that between September 25, YR-2, when the police first examined the car, and October 14, YR-2, when Leslie Roman examined the car, the appearance and condition of the car did not change in any way relevant to the accident reconstruction of Ryan Foster or Leslie Roman. The parties further agree, in addition to being irrelevant, that any discrepancies in the appearance of the YR-3 Impala between the police photos and Leslie Roman's photos did not occur

through the fault of either party. Both parties waive all objections to the authenticity of the photographs and waive all objections to the captions of the photographs.

5. Danny Dawson weighed 160 pounds on September 25, YR-2.

6. Danny Dawson suffered from no medical or psychological conditions that impacted Danny Dawson's ability to drive a motor vehicle on September 25, YR-2.

7. Exhibit 15, the Chuggie's Drink Menu, is the menu that was in use at Chuggie's on September 24 and 25, YR-2.

_____/s/_____   _____/s/_____

Attorney for the State of Nita   Attorney for Defendant

IN THE CIRCUIT COURT OF DARROW COUNTY, NITA

CRIMINAL COURT DIVISION

STATE OF NITA,

    Plaintiff,

v.

DANNY DAWSON,

    Defendant.

CASE NO. CR-YR-1-1030

JURY INSTRUCTIONS

Under the evidence presented to you in this case, you shall find the Defendant, Danny Dawson, not guilty under these Instructions unless you believe beyond a reasonable doubt from the evidence that Danny Dawson is guilty of one or more of the following offenses:

1. Murder, as set out in Instruction No. 1;

    OR

2. Manslaughter, as set out in Instruction No. 2;

    OR

3. Negligent Homicide, as set out in Instruction No. 3;

    AND/OR

4. Operating a Motor Vehicle While under the Influence of Alcohol, as set out in Instruction No. 4.

INSTRUCTION NO. 1: MURDER

You will find the defendant, Danny Dawson, guilty of Murder under this Instruction if, and only if, you believe beyond a reasonable doubt from the evidence all of the following:

A. That in this county on or about September 25, YR-2, Danny Dawson killed Vanessa Sullivan by injuring her in a motor vehicle;

[handwritten: reckless conduct that created grave risk of death + under circumstances w/ extreme indiff to human life]

AND

B. That in so doing, Danny Dawson was <u>recklessly engaging in conduct that created a grave risk</u> <u>of death to another and thereby caused the death of Vanessa Sullivan under circumstances</u> manifesting an extreme indifference to human life.

If you find the defendant, Danny Dawson, guilty under this Instruction, you will say so by your verdict.

INSTRUCTION NO. 2: MANSLAUGHTER

If you do not find the defendant, Danny Dawson, guilty under Instruction No. 1, you will find the defendant guilty of Manslaughter under this Instruction if, and only if, you believe beyond a reasonable doubt from the evidence all of the following:

A. That in this county on or about September 25, YR-2, Danny Dawson killed <u>Vanessa Sullivan</u> by <u>injuring her in a motor vehicle</u>;

AND

B. That in so doing, Danny Dawson was acting <u>recklessly</u>.

If you find the defendant, Danny Dawson, guilty under this Instruction, you will say so by your verdict.

INSTRUCTION NO. 3: NEGLIGENT HOMICIDE

If you do not find the defendant, Danny Dawson, guilty under Instruction No. 1 or Instruction No. 2, you will find the defendant guilty of <u>Negligent Homicide</u> under this Instruction if, and only if, you believe beyond a reasonable doubt from the evidence all of the following:

A. That in this county on or about September 25, YR-2, Danny Dawson killed Vanessa Sullivan by injuring her in a motor vehicle;

AND

B. That in so doing, Danny Dawson was acting negligently.

If you find the defendant, Danny Dawson, guilty under this Instruction, you will say so by your verdict.

INSTRUCTION NO. 4: OPERATING A MOTOR VEHICLE WHILE UNDER THE INFLUENCE OF ALCOHOL

You will find the defendant, Danny Dawson, guilty of Operating a Motor Vehicle While Under the Influence of Alcohol if, and only if, you believe beyond a reasonable doubt from the evidence all of the following:

A. That in this county on or about September 25, YR-2, Danny Dawson operated a motor vehicle;

AND

B. Danny Dawson's ability to operate a motor vehicle was impaired by alcohol or other drugs.

If you find the defendant, Danny Dawson, guilty under this Instruction, you will say so by your verdict.

INSTRUCTION NO. 5: DEFINITIONS

can we focus on consuously? alcohol made it not conscious?

Recklessly. A person acts recklessly with respect to a material element of an offense when he consciously disregards a substantial and unjustifiable risk that the material element exists or will result from his conduct. The risk must be of such a nature and degree that considering the nature and purpose of the actor's conduct and the circumstances known to him, its disregard involves a gross deviation from the standard of conduct that a law-abiding person would observe in the actor's situation.

Negligently. A person acts negligently with respect to a material element of an offense when he should be aware of a substantial and unjustifiable risk that the material element exists or will result from his conduct. The risk must be of such a nature and degree that the actor's failure to perceive it, considering the nature and purpose of his conduct and the circumstances known to him, involves a gross deviation from the standard of care that a reasonable person would observe in the actor's situation.

Intoxication means a disturbance of mental or physical capacities resulting from the introduction of substances into the body.

Voluntary Intoxication means intoxication caused by substances that the defendant knowingly introduces into his body, the tendency of which to cause intoxication he knows or ought to know (unless he introduces them pursuant to medical advice or under such threat of physical force against him that a person in the defendant's situation could not have been expected to resist, provided that the defendant did not, either intentionally or wantonly, place himself in a situation in which it was probable that he would be subjected to coercion).

Evidence means:

- first, the sworn testimony of witnesses, both on direct and cross-examination, regardless of who called the witness;

- second, the exhibits admitted by the court;

- third, any facts to which the lawyers have agreed or stipulated or that the court has directed you to find;

- fourth, circumstantial evidence, which is evidence from which you may logically find other facts according to common knowledge and experience.

None of these types of evidence is necessarily better or worse than another. Any type of evidence can prove a fact. Anything you may have seen or heard outside the courtroom is not evidence, although you may take into account matters of your common knowledge and your observations and experience in the affairs of life.

Reasonable doubt means a doubt based upon reason and common sense. It is a doubt for which a reason can be given, arising from a fair and rational consideration of the evidence or lack of evidence. It is not a doubt that is based on mere guesswork or speculation. A doubt that arises merely from sympathy or from fear to return a verdict of guilt is not a reasonable doubt. A reasonable doubt is not a doubt such as may be used to escape the responsibility of a decision.

INSTRUCTION NO. 7: ARGUMENTS AND REMARKS OF COUNSEL

Remarks of the attorneys are not evidence. If the remarks suggested certain facts not in evidence, disregard the suggestion. However, you are to consider carefully the closing arguments of the attorneys. Ultimately, you must draw your own conclusions from the evidence and decide upon your verdict according to the evidence, under the instructions given you by the court.

INSTRUCTION NO. 8: PRESUMPTION OF INNOCENCE

The law presumes a defendant to be innocent of a crime, and the indictment shall not be considered as evidence or as having any weight against him. You shall find the defendant not guilty unless you are satisfied from the evidence alone and beyond a reasonable doubt that the defendant is guilty. If upon the whole case you have a reasonable doubt as to guilt, you shall find the defendant not guilty.

INSTRUCTION NO. 9: RIGHT TO REMAIN SILENT

The defendant is not compelled to testify, and the fact that a defendant does not cannot be used as an inference of guilt. If, however, a defendant does testify, you shall judge his credibility per Instruction No. 10.

INSTRUCTION NO. 10: CREDIBILITY OF WITNESSES

It is the duty of the jury to scrutinize and weigh the testimony of witnesses and to determine the effect of the evidence as a whole. You are the sole judges of the credibility—that is, the believability—of the witnesses and of the weight to be given to their testimony.

In determining the credibility of each witness and the weight you give to the testimony of each witness, consider these factors:

- whether the witness has an interest or lack of interest in the result of this trial;

- the witness's conduct, appearance, and demeanor on the witness stand;

- the clearness or lack of clearness of the witness's recollections;

- the opportunity the witness had for observing and for knowing the matters the witness testified about;

- the reasonableness of the witness's testimony;

- the apparent intelligence of the witness;

- bias or prejudice, if any has been shown;

- possible motives for falsifying testimony; and

- all other facts and circumstances during the trial that tend either to support or discredit the testimony.

Then give to the testimony of each witness the weight you believe it should receive.

There is no magic way for you to evaluate the testimony; instead, you should use your common sense and experience.

INSTRUCTION NO. 11: UNANIMOUS VERDICT

The verdict of the jury must be unanimous as to guilty or not guilty, and it must be signed by one of you as foreperson.

DATE: _____   _____

JUDGE

VERDICT UNDER INSTRUCTION NO. 1: MURDER

We, the Jury, find the Defendant, Danny Dawson, NOT GUILTY under Instruction No. 1.

_____

FOREPERSON

We, the Jury, find the Defendant, Danny Dawson, GUILTY under Instruction No. 1.

_____

FOREPERSON

VERDICT UNDER INSTRUCTION NO. 2: MANSLAUGHTER

We, the Jury, find the Defendant, Danny Dawson, NOT GUILTY under Instruction No. 2.

_____

FOREPERSON

We, the Jury, find the Defendant, Danny Dawson, GUILTY under Instruction No. 2.

_____

FOREPERSON

VERDICT UNDER INSTRUCTION NO. 3: NEGLIGENT HOMICIDE

We, the Jury, find the Defendant, Danny Dawson, NOT GUILTY under Instruction No. 3.

_____

FOREPERSON

We, the Jury, find the Defendant, Danny Dawson, GUILTY under Instruction No. 3.

_____

FOREPERSON

VERDICT UNDER INSTRUCTION NO. 4: OPERATING A MOTOR VEHICLE WHILE UNDER INFLUENCE OF ALCOHOL

We, the Jury, find the Defendant, Danny Dawson, NOT GUILTY under Instruction No. 4.

_____

FOREPERSON

We, the Jury, find the Defendant, Danny Dawson, GUILTY under Instruction No. 4.

_____

FOREPERSON

Exhibit 1b

```
NGK WIRELESS COMMUNICATIONS
TRANSCRIPT OF AUDIO TRANSMISSION VOICE MESSAGE RETRIEVAL
FROM: ACCOUNT 555-272-7376
TO:   ACCOUNT 555-715-5507

DATE OF TRANSMISSION: SEPTEMBER 25, YR-2
TIME OF TRANSMISSION: 0057 HOURS

[BEGIN MESSAGE]
```

MUSIC: *ARTIST NOT IDENTIFIED*

```
VOICE ONE: HI DAD, IT'S ME. VANESSA
```
INAUDIBLE MUMBLE . . . KEEP IT DOWN . . .
INAUDIBLE MUMBLE . . . TALK TO MY DAD
```
                SORRY DAD, UH, ANYWAY, HI, UH IT'S ME, VANESSA
                AND, UM, I'M SORRY. I JUST SAID THAT, DIDN'T I
                UM, SORRY. ANYWAY, I WAS JUST CALLING TO LET YOU
                KNOW THAT WE'RE GONNA BE A FEW MINUTES
OTHER VOICES:   INAUDIBLE MUMBLE
VOICE ONE: DANNY WHAT ARE YOU DOING, STAY ON THE ROAD
                UM, SORRY DAD, I'M SORRY
                WE'RE FINE, AH, DANNY IS JUST BEING AN IDIOT
                UM ANYWAYS
                WE'RE FINE AND WE SHOULD BE THERE SHORTLY
                UM, BUT ANYWAY, I WAS ASK-
                CALLING, SORRY, CALLING TO ASK IF YOU
                WOULDN'T MIND IF YOU COULD LEAVE THE GARAGE DOOR
                OPEN BECAUSE IT HAS BEEN POURING DOWN RAIN
                AND I-
                IT'S GONNA BE RIDICULOUS INAUDIBLE
                TRY AND WALK IN
                UM, AND I JUST WANNA LET YOU KNOW THAT I LOVE YOU
                AND WE SHOULD BE THERE SOON
                UM, I'LL TALK TO YOU LAT-
                DANNY
UNIDENTIFIED NOISE
UNIDENTIFIED SCREAM

[END OF MESSAGE]
```

```
*************Chuggie's************

09/24/YR-2    000001 BILL #0114
6:45 PM                 PAT0012
CARD TYPE      ACCT NUMBER
VISA           xxxxxxxxxxxx4170
TRANSACTION APPROVED
AUTHORIZATION #:        040017
REFERENCE:             62175012

Guest 1

1 Iron IPA              $3.50
1 Deluxe Nachos         $7.99
1 Whiskey & Ginger      $3.00
1 Whiskey & Ginger      $3.00
1 Whiskey & Ginger      $3.00

Items 5
Total                  $20.49
Tip                     $4.00
Total                  $24.49


X    Danny Dawson

**********MERCHANT COPY*********
```

Nachos

4 drinks purchased on this receipt

Exhibit 2b

```
*************Chuggie's************

09/25/YR-2    000001  BILL #0217
12:37 AM           PAT0012
CARD TYPE      ACCT NUMBER
VISA           xxxxxxxxxxxx4170
TRANSACTION APPROVED
AUTHORIZATION #:      040017
REFERENCE:           62178940

Guest 1

1 Big Horn Burger
w/extra ketchup          $10.49
1 Whiskey - Black Label  $8.00
2 Screwdriver @ $3.00    $6.00
1 XL Cheese Fries        $7.99
2 Lemon Drop Shot @ $5.00
                         $10.00
1 Nita Brown Pint        $2.50
1 Soda                   $1.50
2 Screwdriver @ $3.00    $6.00
1 Soda Refill            $0.50
1 Soda Refill            $0.50
2 Screwdriver @ $3.00    $6.00
1 Soda Refill            $0.50
2 Screwdriver @ $3.00    $6.00
1 Soda Refill            $0.50
2 Screwdriver @ $3.00    $6.00
1 Tequila Sunrise        $3.00
1 Soda Refill            $0.50
1 Soda Refill            $0.50

Items 27
Total                    $76.48
Tip                      $20.00
Total                    $96.48

X    Danny Dawson

*********MERCHANT COPY*********
```

Handwritten annotations:
- Burger, XL cheese fries
- ‖‖‖ ‖‖‖ ‖‖‖ 15 drinks purchased on this receipt

```
*************Chuggie's************

09/25/YR-2    000001 BILL #0215
12:35 AM              PAT0012
CARD TYPE     ACCT NUMBER
VISA          xxxxxxxxxxxx6169
TRANSACTION APPROVED
AUTHORIZATION #:        040017
REFERENCE:             62178938

Guest 1

1 Grand Caesar Salad
        w/ chicken @ $2.00    $11.99
1 Horse's Head Sauvignon Blanc
            (Glass)           $6.00
1 Low Plateau Merlot (Glass)  $4.00
1 Low Plateau Merlot (Glass)  $4.00

Items 4
Total                        $25.99
Tip                           $4.00
Total                        $29.99


X     Vanessa Sullivan

**********MERCHANT COPY**********
```

3 drinks purchased on this

Exhibit 3

Department of Transportation
National Highway Traffic Safety Administration
Conforming Products List Of Evidential Breath Measurement Devices

Issued August 7, YR-2

Alcohol Countermeasure Systems Corp. Mississauga, Ontario, Canada:
 Alert J3AD*
 Alert J4X.ec
 PBA3000C
BAC Systems, Inc., Ontario, Canada: Breath Analysis Computer*
CAMEC Ltd., North Shields, Tyne and Ware, England: IR Breath Analyzer*
CMI, Inc., Owensboro, KY:
 Intoxilyzer Model:
 200
 200D
 300
 400
 400PA
 1400
 4011*
 4011A*
 4011AS*
 4011AS–A*
 4011AS–AQ*
 4011 AW*
 4011A27–10100*
 4011A27–10100 with filter*
 5000
 5000 (w/Cal. Vapor Re-Circ.)
 5000 (w/3/8" ID Hose option)
 5000CD
 5000CD/FG5
 5000EN
 5000 (CAL DOJ)
 5000VA
 8000
 PAC 1200*
 S–D2
 S–D5
Draeger Safety, Inc., Durango, CO:
 Alcotest Model:
 6510
 7010*
 7110*
 7110 MKIII
 7110 MKIII–C
 7410
 7410 Plus
 Breathalyzer Model:
 900*
 900A*
 900BG*
 7410
 7410–II

Gall's Inc., Lexington, KY: Alcohol Detection System—A.D.S. 500
Intoximeters, Inc., St. Louis, MO:
> Photo Electric Intoximeter*
> GC Intoximeter MK II*
> GC Intoximeter MK IV*
> Auto Intoximeter*
> Intoximeter Model:
> > 3000*
> > 3000 (rev B1)*
> > 3000 (rev B2)*
> > 3000 (rev B2A)*
> > 3000 (rev B2A) w/FM option*
> > 3000 (Fuel Cell)*
> > 3000 D*
> > 3000 DFC*
> Alcomonitor CC.
> Alco-Sensor III
> Alco-Sensor III (Enhanced with Serial Numbers above 1,200,000
> Alco-Sensor IV
> Alco-Sensor IV–XL
> Alco-Sensor AZ
> Alco-Sensor FST
> RBT–AZ
> RBT III
> RBT III–A
> RBT IV
> RBT IV with CEM (cell enhancement module)
> Intox EC/IR
> Intox EC/IR II
> Portable Intox EC/IR
Komyo Kitagawa, Kogyo, K.K.:
> Alcolyzer DPA–2*
> Breath Alcohol Meter PAM 101B*
Lifeloc Technologies, Inc., (formerly Lifeloc, Inc.), Wheat Ridge, CO:
> PBA 3000B
> PBA 3000–P*
> PBA 3000C
> Alcohol Data Sensor
> Phoenix
> FC 10
> FC 20
Lion Laboratories, Ltd., Cardiff, Wales, UK:
> Alcolmeter Model:
> > 300
> > 400
> > SD–2*
> > EBA*
> Intoxilyzer Model:
> > 200
> > 200D
> > 1400
> > 5000 CD/FG5
> > 5000 EN
> > 1400
National Draeger, Inc., Durango, CO:
> Alcotest Model:
> > 7010*
> > 7110*
> > 7110 MKIII
> > 7110 MKIII-C
> > 7410
> > 7410 Plus

Breathalyzer Model:
  900*
  900A*
  900BG*
  7410
  7410–II
National Patent Analytical Systems, Inc., Mansfield, OH:
 BAC DataMaster (with or without the Delta–1 accessory)
 BAC Verifier DataMaster (with or without the Delta–1 accessory)
 DataMaster cdm (with or without the Delta–1 accessory)
Omicron Systems, Palo Alto, CA:
 Intoxilyzer Model:
  4011*
  4011AW*
Plus 4 Engineering, Minturn, CO: 5000 Plus4*
Seres, Paris, France:
 Alco Master
 Alcopro
Siemans-Allis, Cherry Hill, NJ:
 Alcomat*
 Alcomat F*
Smith and Wesson Electronics, Springfield, MA:
 Breathalyzer Model:
  900*
  900A*
  1000*
  YR-12*
 YR-12 (non-Humidity Sensor)*
Sound-Off, Inc., Hudsonville, MI:
 AlcoData
 Seres Alco Master
 Seres Alcopro
Stephenson Corp.: Breathalyzer 900*
U.S. Alcohol Testing, Inc./Protection Devices, Inc., Rancho Cucamonga, CA:
 Alco-Analyzer 1000
 Alco-Analyzer YR-12
 Alco-Analyzer 2100
Verax Systems, Inc., Fairport, NY:
 BAC Verifier*
 BAC Verifier Datamaster
 BAC Verifier Datamaster II*

*Instruments marked with an asterisk (*) are instruments tested at 0.000, 0.050, 0.101, and 0.151 BAC. Instruments not marked with an asterisk were tested at BACs = 0.000, 0.020, 0.040, 0.080, and 0.160. All instruments meet the current Model Specifications currently in effect and also meet the current Model Specifications for Screening Devices to Measure Alcohol in Bodily Fluids.

This list is a complete, exclusive, and accurate copy of the instruments currently acceptable for use by local, state, and federal law enforcement. Any device not explicitly included on this list does not meet NHTSA standards and may not be used.

Exhibit 4

NITA POLICE DEPARTMENT
FORENSICS SECTION
INTOXILYZER 8000 OPERATOR'S CHECKLIST

(Please Print)

09/25/YR-2 _____   _____Foster_____
Test Date   Arresting Officer

Dawson, Danny N._____   _____ 5437W
Driver's Name (Last, First, Middle)   Arresting Officer's Badge #

Operational Checklist

X **Pre-test observational period:** The operator is certain that the subject has not ingested any substance by mouth (eating, drinking, smoking, etc.), eructated, vomited, or regurgitated liquid from the stomach to the mouth for at least fifteen (15) minutes before the testing commences.

Observer Name (Print): _____

Start pre-observation time: _01:30_____   End pre-observation time: _____01:45____

Timepiece used: __ Instrument   X Wristwatch __ Other: _____

X **Test start:** When the instrument display reads "Ready," push "Start Test" to begin testing sequence.

X Enter the operator's information and code.

X Enter the subject's information.

X Select Test Mode

X Instruct subject on how to give a proper sample; have subject give first sample.

X Continue to observe for two (2) minutes.

X Instruct subject to give second sample; make sure machine acknowledges sample acceptance.

X Enter comments (if any) about the subject test.

X Press "Print" and remove test result from printer.

Comments:_____

_____

50-001444_____   _____ Nita Center
Instrument Serial #   Location

AVERY SMITH_____   _____ A/S
Operator's Name (Print)   Operator's Signature

FORENSICS_____   _____ 540177
Operator's Department   Operator's License

Exhibit 5

Nita Center Department of Corrections

Breath Test Operator's Report

Name: __Danny Dawson__   Weight: __160__   DOB: __9/29/YR-25__

Do you have anything in your mouth at this time?   YES   (NO)
If so, please remove it now.

Implied Consent Read: (YES)   NO

Attempted to Contact Attorney: (YES)   NO   Made Contact: (YES)   NO

Mirandized: Understood?   (YES)   NO   Waived: (YES)   NO

Interview:

Have you been drinking? __Yes__   What? __Mixed drinks__   How much? __A drink an (hour)__

I drink per hour since 2 pm

When did you begin? __2:00 p.m.__   Where were you?
__Chuggie's__

When did you have your last drink? __an hour or so ago__   When did you get
arrested? __a half hour ago__

Where were you going? __Vanessa's Home__

Have you used any drugs? YES (NO)   Have you been using marijuana? YES (NO)

Are you taking medication? YES (NO)   If so, what? _____

Do you have diabetes? YES (NO)   Are you taking insulin? YES (NO)

Are you hurt in any way? (YES) NO   In what way? __Banged up from accident__

Have you been to the dentist or doctor today? YES (NO)

I am requesting that you submit to a test of your:

A. (Breath)   B. Blood   C. Urine

Refused?

A.   Yes   B. (No)

Blood test: Drawn by: _____ N/A _____

Physical appearance (Clothing, tattoos, hygiene, etc.):

Nothing of note. _____

_____

_____

Remarks on speech, walk, and observations of subject:

_____ Consistent with moderate to heavy drinking. Stumbled slightly when _____

attempting to walk. Spoke extremely deliberately. _____

_____

_____

_____

Test Made by: (Print) ___Avery Smith_____ Badge #: _____

Signature: _____ /s/ AS _____

Witnessed by (if applicable): _____ N/A _____ Badge #: _____

I hereby confirm that this form was accurately completed.

Signature: /s/ Danny Dawson _____

Exhibit 6

NITA Center Police Department
Department of Forensics
Breath Test Report

```
TEST DATE: 09/25/YR-2
INSTRUMENT: INTOXILYZER - ALCOHOL ANALYZER MODEL 8000
SN#: 50-001444   TEST LOCATION: NITA CENTER

SUBJECT NAME:        DANNY DAWSON
SUBJECT LICENSE:     DAWSD137ND
SUBJECT DOB:         09/29/YR-25
```

TEST	%BAC	STATUS	TIME
AIR BLANK	0.000	PASS	01:51
DIAGNOSTIC OK		PASS	01:51
AIR BLANK	0.000	PASS	01:52
SUBJECT SAMPLE	0.194	OBTAINED	01:52
AIR BLANK	0.000	PASS	01:53
AIR BLANK	0.000	PASS	01:55
SUBJECT SAMPLE	0.191	OBTAINED	01:56
AIR BLANK	0.000	PASS	01:57
CONTROL SAMPLE	0.084	PASS	01:57
AIR BLANK	0.000	PASS	01:58

```
** EXPECTED VALUE FOR CONTROL: 0.085 **
```

TEST RESULT: 0.19 ← *Result is 0.19 one hour after last drink*

```
ADDITIONAL INFORMATION:  ANY OBSERVATIONS MADE BY THE OPERATOR DURING
THE TESTING MAY BE RECORDED IN THE COMMENT SECTION BELOW.      >0.08
NOTES:    NONE.

OPERATOR'S NAME:     AVERY SMITH
LICENSE #:           540177
DEPARTMENT:          FORENSICS
METHOD:              TWO SAMPLE
```

THE ABOVE-NAMED INDIVIDUAL HAS SATISFACTORILY MET THE REQUIREMENTS OF
THE NITA CENTER DEPARTMENT OF FORENSICS IN THE CHEMICAL ANALYSIS OF A
PERSON'S BREATH AND IS APPROVED TO OPERATE THE ABOVE-LISTED EQUIPMENT
USING THE ABOVE-LISTED METHOD AS SPECIFIED BY THE NITA CENTER DEPARTMENT
OF FORENSICS.

```
COMMENTS: NONE
SIGNED:_____AS_____
```

Exhibit 7

Alcohol Ingestion and the Human Body
By Dr. Becky Benton and Dr. Eve Carman

This list of the psychological and physiological effects of alcohol consumption is based on work that the authors performed at the University of Washington Medical Center over the last two decades. All information contained herein has been corroborated with several different studies run by doctors at seven different accredited medical schools across the country. This list is considered to be the authority on this subject among those in the scientific and medical communities. These effects are true across gender, age, race, ethnicity, and all other demographic factors. Some individuals may appear to be more or less intoxicated to the general observer than their BAC indicates, but this is the exception rather than the rule.

Danny is in this zone @ 0.19

All numbers are % BAC.

0.01–0.05	Average individual appears normal
0.03–0.12	Mild euphoria, talkativeness, decreased inhibitions, decreased attention, impaired judgment
0.09–0.25	Emotional instability, loss of critical judgment, impairment of memory and comprehension, decreased sensory response, mild decrease in muscular coordination
0.18–0.30	Confusion, dizziness, exaggerated emotions, impaired visual perception, decreased pain sensation, impaired balance, staggering gait, slurred speech, moderate coordination impairment
0.27–0.40	Apathy, impaired consciousness, stupor, significantly decreased response to stimulation, severe coordination impairment, inability to stand or walk, vomiting, incontinence of urine and feces
0.35-0.50	Unconsciousness, depressed or abolished reflexes, abnormal body temperature, coma; above 0.40 death from respiratory paralysis

Exhibit 8a

DR. ASHLEY NORTON
CURRICULUM VITAE

Defense
medical expert

Education

Bachelor of Science	Chemistry	Brown University	YR-26
Masters	Forensic Science	Johns Hopkins University	YR-22
Doctorate	Forensic Science	Johns Hopkins University	YR-17

Employment History

Professor of Medicine	Nita State University	YR-7 – Present
Adjunct Professor, Experimental Alcohol Research	Nita State University	YR-11 – YR-7
Alcohol Program Coordinator	Nita Department of Forensics	YR-17 – YR-7
Breath Testing Specialist	Maryland Department of Forensics	YR-24 – YR-17
Research Assistant	Chemistry Dept., Massachusetts Institute of Technology	YR-26 – YR-24

Positions Held

| President, American Board of Forensic Toxicology | YR-2 – Present |
| Member, Drug Testing Advisory Board of the United States Health & Human Services Department | YR-7 – YR-3 |

Professional Training

Breathalyzer Operator	(Intoxilyzer 5000, R, 8000)	Current
Breathalyzer Technician	(Intoxilyzer 5000, R, 8000)	Current
Alcohol Pharmacology	University of Nita	YR-24

Professional Associations

American Board of Clinical Chemistry
Nita Association of Medicolegal Alcohol Researchers
National Safety Council Committee on Alcohol and Other Drugs

Publications (selected)

Huang, Y. and Norton, A. "Applications of the Widmark Formula: Today's Chemistry." *Ethanol and Forensics Journal*, YR-2, 2, 51–72.

Norton, A. and Dubowski, K. "Breath Alcohol Research and Analysis: Biological Factors." *North American Forensics Review*, YR-3, 3, 54–69.

Norton, A. and Jones, AW. "Temperature Fluctuations During Exhalation in Breath Alcohol Testing." *J of Ethanol Studies*, YR-2, 1, 24–43.

Norton, A., Stillman, E., and Cullen, M. "Variations in the Blood:Breath Partition and Breath Alcohol Testing." *American Medical Journal*, YR-6, 54, 303–17.

Norton, A., Stillman, E. and Cullen, M. "Further studies into the Blood:breath Partition Ratio." *American Medical Journal*, YR-5, 55, 312–26.

Tuchler M. and Norton, A. "Measuring Breath Alcohol for Use in Legal Proceedings: Variability of Breath-Test Instruments." *American Medicolegal Journal*, YR-14, 26, 1478–91.

Yao, S. and Norton, A. "The Blood:Breath Partition Ratio in Native Japanese." *Intra-Canadian Medical Journal*, YR-9, 45, 124–52.

CURRICULUM VITAE
LESLIE ROMAN, PE

defense accident reconst. expert

EDUCATION

YR-19	**University of Texas—Austin**
	Bachelor of Science in Mechanical Engineering

EXPERIENCE

YR-9 – Present	**Expert Accident Reconstruction Inc.**
	Principal Engineer/Owner
	Nita Center, Nita
	Vehicle Accident Reconstructionist
YR-14 – YR-9	**Global Motors Manufacturing Corporation**
	Engineering Development Center
	Product Liability Investigator
YR-19 – YR-14	**Nita Department of Transportation**
	Nita Center, Nita
	Traffic Engineer

PROFESSIONAL CERTIFICATIONS

Professional Engineer **PE**

Accreditation Commission for Traffic Accident Reconstructionists **ACTAR**

Crash Data Retrieval (CDR) System Operator Certification

Certified Fire and Explosion Investigator **CFEI**

Certified Vehicle Fire Investigator **CVFI**

CONTINUING EDUCATION

YR-2   Applied Vehicle Dynamics—Society of Automotive Engineers

YR-3   Commercial Vehicle Accident Reconstruction

YR-4   Rollover Criteria for SUVs in Emergency Steering Maneuvers

YR-5   Evaluating a Nighttime Driver Response

YR-5   Human Factors in Traffic Accident Reconstruction—University of North Florida

YR-6   Crash Data Recorder Operator Certification—Collision Safety Institute

YR-7   Tire and Wheel Safety Issues—Society of Automotive Engineers

YR-7   Investigation of Motorcycle Crashes

YR-8   Investigation of Pedestrian and Bicycle Collisions

YR-9   Traffic Accident Reconstruction II—Northwestern University

YR-9   Traffic Accident Reconstruction I—Northwestern University

AFFILIATIONS

Society of Automotive Engineers (SAE)

Accreditation Commission for Traffic Accident Reconstructionists (ACTAR)

National Association of Traffic Accident Reconstructionists and Investigators (NATARI)

National Association of Fire Investigators (NAFI)

OTHER

YR-3   Full Scale Vehicle Crash Testing—ARC/CSI Crash Conference

YR-3   Instructor—Street Survival Teen Driving School

YR-4   Instructor—Vehicle Accident Reconstruction for non-Engineers

YR-4   Motorcycle Crash Testing—University of North Florida

YR-4   Pedestrian and Bicycle Collision Field Tests—University of North Florida

YR-5   Perception and Reaction Time Field Tests—University of North Florida

YR-5   Nighttime Visibility Field Testing—University of North Florida

YR-6   Instructor—Automotive Technology for Passenger Cars

YR-7   ARC/CSI Crash Conference

DR. AVERY SMITH
CURRICULUM VITAE

[handwritten: Prosecution / Director Nita Dept. of Forensics]

Education

- BS   Biochemistry   Gonzaga   YR-36
- MS   Public Administration   Seattle University   YR-33
- MPH   Biostatistics   University of Washington   YR-30
- PhD   Biostatistics   University of Washington   YR-30

Employment

- Director   Nita Department of Forensics   YR-17–Present
- Director, Toxicology Department   Nita Department of Forensics   YR-22–YR-17
- Breath Testing Specialist   Nita Department of Forensics   YR-30–Present
- Toxicology Internship   MidToxx, LLC.   YR-36–YR-35

Positions Held

- Chairman Emeritus, Board of Tests for
  Alcohol and Drug Influence of the State of Nita   YR-11–Present
- State Director Emeritus of Tests for
  Alcohol and Drug Influence of the State of Nita   YR-7–Present

Professional Training

- Breathalyzer Operator   (Intoxilyzer 5000, R, 8000)   current
- Breathalyzer Technician   (Intoxilyzer 5000, R, 8000)   current
- Breathalyzer Instructor   (Intoxilyzer 5000, R, 8000)   current
- Breathalyzer Calibration   (Intoxilyzer 5000, R, 8000)   current
- Supervision for Breath Tests   (Intoxilyzer 5000, R, 8000)   current

Professional Associations

- Nita Association of Forensic Scientists
- National Safety Council on Alcohol and Other Drugs
- American Academy of Forensic Scientists—Toxicology Section

Publications (selected)

- Buchinski, L. and Smith, A. "Correctly Administering Breath Alcohol Testing." *Journal of Forensic Science*, YR-13, 44, 91–107.
- Robie, J. and Smith, A. "Mouth Alcohol: The Significance of Time." *Journal of Ethanol Testing*, YR-5, 15, 47–61.
- Smith, A. "Forensic Application of the Intoxilyzer 8000." *Nita Law Enforcement Review*, YR-7, 5, 15–23.

- Smith, A. and Cramer, E. "Effects of Ethanol Intoxication on the Human Body: A Forensic Scientists Guide." *Journal of Forensic Science*, YR-3, 54, 214–30.
- Smith, A. and Harmon, A. "Alcohol and Driving Impairment." *Journal of Forensic Science*, YR-11, 46, 134–42.
- Smith, A., Harmon, A., Strathern, E. "Prevalence of Drug Use Among Tractor-Trailer Drivers." *Journal of Highway Safety*, YR-9, 15, 92–107.

Exhibit 9

NITA CENTER POLICE DEPARTMENT

FATAL CRASH TEAM

TRAFFIC COLLISION REPORT

October 11, YR-2

FCT CASE NUMBER: 061293

FCT TEAM: 3

FCT INVESTIGATOR: RYAN FOSTER

FCT CASE: 061293

Date: September 25, YR-2

Location: Canyon Road in Nita Center

FCT Investigating Officer: Ryan Foster

Narrative

The Fatal Crash Team (FCT) was requested to assist in the investigation of a single-vehicle fatal crash at approximately 1:00 a.m. on September 25, YR-2, on Canyon Road near 5234 Canyon Road in Nita Center, Nita.

The involved vehicle is a YR-3 Chevrolet Impala sedan, VIN: 1G8ZK55729Z103114. The vehicle was registered to Vanessa Sullivan, whom I later learned was the right front-seat passenger.

Danny Dawson admitted to driving the vehicle, but was unable to provide details as to how the crash occurred. Dawson recalled losing control of the vehicle and striking a tree. Dawson was transported to the police station for testing to determine Dawson's blood alcohol content (BAC).

The front of the vehicle was in contact with Nita Center Utility Pole 2183, and the right side of the vehicle was against a large tree approximately three feet in diameter. The rear tires were on the west fog line. Once the rain stopped, the final rest position of the tires was marked with paint prior to the car being removed from the scene.

There was no alcohol or drug paraphernalia visible in the vehicle at the scene.

The right front seat occupant remained in the vehicle and was deceased upon my arrival. Another passenger, Taylor Hopson, was the rear seat passenger and was dazed, but conscious. Hopson was wearing a seat belt when I arrived. Hopson appeared to have suffered cuts and bruises as a result of the crash.

London Bennett, who resides at 5234 Canyon Road, observed part of the incident. Bennett recalled seeing the vehicle steer first one direction and then the other before leaving the road and striking the tree.

I attempted to photograph and document all evidence at the scene. Due to the heavy rains, limited roadway evidence was available and/or visible.

The vehicle was removed from the scene, and the roadway reopened at approximately 3:15 a.m.

On September 25, YR-2, I returned to the crash scene and surveyed the roadway, guard rail, utility pole, and tree. I also identified rutting alongside the eastern edge of pavement in the curve immediately preceding (south of) the crash site. The rutting was approximately 124 feet in length. The distance from the northernmost end of the rutting to the impacted tree was 146 feet.

On October 2, YR-2, I made a study of the vehicle. I measured and documented the vehicle damage. The maximum deformation on the right passenger door was approximately twenty-four inches laterally. The front bumper was deformed into a V-shaped pattern with a maximum deformation of approximately eight inches.

The Event Data Recorder (EDR), commonly referred to as a "black box" was located under the right front passenger seat. I examined the EDR and found that it had been destroyed in the collision, and consequently, I could not collect any data from it. I removed the EDR from the vehicle and stored it in Nita PD evidence.

On October 7, YR-2, the trees along the west side of the roadway were removed by Nita Center Municipal Utility District. On October 9, YR-2, the guard rail on the west side of the road was extended approximately 105 feet to the south.

The Fatal Crash Scene (FCT) Diagram is attached to this report.

(Continued on next page)

FCT CASE: 061293

DATE: September 25, YR-2

LOCATION: Canyon Road in Nita Center

FCT Investigating Officer: Ryan Foster

NOTE: The following represents the opinions of the above-identified member of the Nita Center Police Department. These opinions are based upon the evidence and information in this case and the education and experience of the individual.

While investigating this case, I examined the scene of the crash and conducted a general vehicle inspection. I used this crash scene survey to assist in a mathematical analysis of the crash. Based on everything that is known at this time, I am of the following opinions.

[handwritten: 35 mph]

1. Analysis indicates Danny Dawson was traveling northbound on Canyon River Road. The posted speed limit on this section of Canyon River Road is thirty-five miles per hour.

2. Dawson was traveling too fast for the rainy conditions on a curved section of the roadway and failed to negotiate the curve. The right side tires exited the east edge of pavement, creating a rut in the grass approximately 124 feet in length.

3. Dawson attempted to re-enter the roadway and overcorrected, causing a complete loss of control. The vehicle traveled 146 feet while spinning and exited the west edge of pavement, striking a utility pole.

4. The collision with the utility pole caused the vehicle to rotate counterclockwise, at which point the right side of the vehicle struck a tree.

5. The drag factors on the grass and a wet section of the roadway were 0.35 and 0.23, respectively. I used a drag sled to measure the drag factors.

[handwritten: travelling 45mph]

6. The vehicle was traveling approximately forty miles per hour when it struck the tree. This is based upon the equivalent speed equation with a twenty-four-inch deformation over a wide area.

[handwritten: 20 mph]

7. The equivalent speed due to damage resulting from striking the utility pole resulting in a frontal deformation of eight inches is twenty miles per hour.

[handwritten: 45mph when hit utility pole]

8. Using the combined speed formula (twenty miles per hour plus forty miles per hour), the speed at impact with the utility pole is forty-five miles per hour.

[handwritten: 66mph when first exited the road]

9. Further using the combined speed formula over distances of 124 feet (grass) and 146 feet (spinning on road), the speed of the vehicle when it first exited the road was sixty-six miles per hour. *[handwritten: 66-35 = 31 mph over speed limit]*

10. The cause of the collision is excessive speed for the roadway and conditions.

Exhibit 10

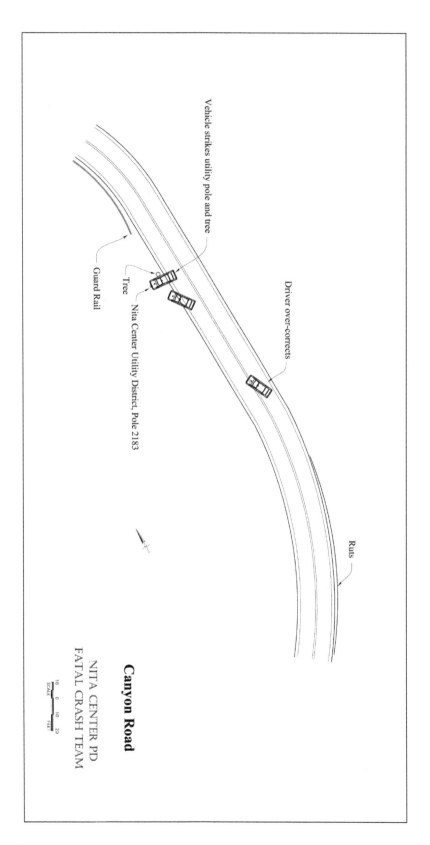

Vehicle strikes utility pole and tree

Driver over-corrects

Guard Rail

Tree

Nita Center Utility District, Pole 2183

Ruts

Canyon Road

NITA CENTER PD
FATAL CRASH TEAM

SCALE
10 0 10 20
FEET

Exhibit 11

<u>**EXPERT ACCIDENT RECONSTRUCTION INC.**</u>
410 MAIN STREET, MIDLANDS CENTER, MIDLANDS

Defendant's Counsel

55 Chambers Avenue

East Hill, Nita

Defense Experts Crash Analysis

     RE: **Danny Dawson**

              Traffic Crash; Canyon Road

              Nita Center, Nita

              File Number: Client File

              EARI Project Number: 10.120A

Dear Counsel:

At your request, on October 14, YR-2, a study and survey were made of the collision site referenced in the above file number, and a study was made of the involved YR-3 Chevrolet Impala. The purpose of the study was to reconstruct the traffic collision. The Nita Center Police Department investigated the collision, and Officer Foster was the investigating officer at the scene. This letter, with the attached photographs and graphics, is the report of my findings and conclusions.

Basis of Analysis

- Study and survey of the collision site (including photographs taken at the scene) on October 14, YR-2

- Examination of the involved vehicle on October 14, YR-2

- Nita Center Police Fatal Crash Team (FCT) Police Report, case number 061293

- Photographs of the crash scene taken by Nita Center Police personnel shortly after the accident

- Affidavit of London Bennett

- Affidavit of Taylor Hopson

Description of the Traffic Crash

According to the police report referenced above, the traffic crash occurred at approximately 1:00 a.m. on September 25, YR-2. The collision site is located on Canyon Road, approximately one mile north of Dry Fork Road in Nita Center, Nita. The incident is reported as a single-vehicle collision that occurred during dark hours with rainy weather conditions.

The vehicle identified by the investigating officer is as follows:

- Vehicle #1: White Chevrolet Impala sedan, VIN: 1G8ZK55729Z103114, owned by Vanessa Sullivan and being operated by Danny Dawson of Nita Center, Nita.

According to the narrative contained within the Police Report, Vehicle #1 was traveling northbound on Canyon River Road when the vehicle exited the east side of the roadway. The driver attempted to re-enter the roadway and lost control of the vehicle, causing the vehicle to exit the west side of the roadway and strike a utility pole and a tree.

Information provided by your office indicates that Danny Dawson stated that Dawson observed a deer in the roadway immediately prior to the loss of control and that Dawson claimed to swerve in an unsuccessful attempt to avoid a collision.

Study of the Crash Site

The crash site is shown in the attached Photographs 1 through 15. Photographs 1 through 7 were taken by the police FCT at the scene shortly after the accident. Photographs 8 through 15 were taken as part of my study and survey of the accident site on October 14, YR-2. In the area of the collision, Canyon Road is an asphalt-surfaced rural roadway oriented generally north-to-south with one travel lane in each direction. The travel lanes are approximately ten feet in width. Opposing lanes of travel are separated by a solid double yellow line. Paved shoulders on each side of the roadway are approximately two feet in width. The road is characterized with various curves and hillcrests. The speed limit on Canyon Road is thirty-five miles per hour.

The collision occurred near 5234 Canyon Road. Northbound traffic experiences a curve to the west (left). Rutting is evident in the grass along the east edge of pavement. The rutting extends approximately 124 feet prior to reentering the roadway. There are no tire marks on the roadway that can be identified as being related to this incident.

A utility pole (ID: Nita Center Utility District, Pole 2183) is positioned approximately eight feet west of the west edge of pavement. Damage to the utility pole is consistent with an impact from a motor vehicle. Numerous trees have been cut down in the area near the utility pole, including the tree impacted by the vehicle. Prior to the collision, the tree impacted by the vehicle was thirty-nine inches in diameter and positioned approximately thirty inches from the edge of the pavement. The general terrain in the area where the vehicle exited the west edge of pavement is characterized by a downhill grade of approximately 40 percent away from the roadway. The distance from the end of the rutting to the utility pole is approximately 144 feet.

Prior to the collision, the guardrail on the west side of the road terminated approximately thirty-two feet north of the utility pole. Subsequent to the collision, the guard rail was extended approximately 105 feet southward to include the area where the vehicle exited the roadway.

Due to the curvature of the roadway immediately preceding the area of impact, the driver's sight distance is limited. A deer crossing sign is present for northbound traffic approximately one mile south of the area of impact. There are no "Curve Ahead" or speed-advisory road signs located within 0.5 miles south of the area of the crash.

Vehicle Study

For the purposes of this report, the driver's side of the vehicle is considered the left and the hood the front. At the time of my study, the vehicle was located at the Nita Center Police Impound Lot. The front of the vehicle exhibits damage consistent with striking a utility pole. The front bumper structure is deformed in a V-shaped pattern, with the maximum deformation of nine inches located near the vehicle centerline. The hood is buckled, and the radiator core support is deformed rearward.

The right side of the vehicle exhibits damage consistent with a near-lateral (sideways) impact with a large tree. The right door, rocker panel, and roof are deformed toward the left. The depth and width of the damaged area are twenty-four inches and forty-two inches, respectively. The vehicle unibody frame is buckled due to the collision. The plastic door trim on the left front door is separated from the vehicle, most likely as a result of the impact.

This vehicle is equipped with an Event Data Recorder (EDR), commonly referred to as a "black box." The EDR in this vehicle contains pre-crash data, including vehicle speed, accelerator pedal position, and brake position. The EDR is normally located under the right front seat. Prior to my study, the EDR was removed from the vehicle and was not available to attempt a download of the data contained within.

Analysis of the Traffic Incident

The collision occurred on Canyon Road approximately one mile north of Dry Fork road in Nita Center, Nita. Danny Dawson was traveling northbound on Canyon Road, negotiating a curve toward the left in an area known to be populated by deer. A deer-crossing sign is present approximately one mile south of the crash location. As Dawson negotiated the curve, a deer became visible in the roadway. Dawson steered to the right to avoid striking the deer, and the right tires of the vehicle drove off the right (east) edge of pavement. The angle at which the rutting departs from the edge of pavement is consistent with being preceded by an evasive maneuver.

Dawson attempted to re-enter the roadway and overcorrected, causing the vehicle to rotate counter-clockwise and exit the west edge of pavement. The front of the vehicle struck a utility pole, and the right front door struck a large tree.

The vehicle exited the west edge of pavement in an area with a grade away from the road of approximately 40 percent. At the time of the collision, the guard rail did not extend far enough to the south to protect vehicles from this severe drop-off. Between the time of the collision and my study on October 14, the guard rail had been extended to include this area.

Numerous trees had been cut down in the area where the vehicle exited the roadway, including the tree struck by the vehicle. This particular tree was located approximately thirty inches from the edge of pavement in an area characterized by narrow lanes and unprotected by a guard rail.

The right side of the vehicle was deformed inward approximately twenty-four inches, with a damage width of forty-two inches. The speed equivalent, due to the energy crushing the side of the vehicle, is thirty-one miles per hour using the energy-conservation method considering impact with a narrow object. The speed equivalent due to the damage at the front of the vehicle striking the utility pole is sixteen miles per hour. Using the combined-speed formula, the speed of the vehicle at impact with the utility pole is thirty-five miles per hour.

[handwritten margin note: 35 mph @ impact w/ pole]

The vehicle traveled approximately 124 feet with the right tires off the roadway, with a friction factor of approximately 0.25. The vehicle then re-entered the road and traveled an additional 144 feet while rotating with a drag factor of approximately 0.1. A low drag factor was used due to the heavy rains and slippery conditions of the road at the time of the crash. Analysis using the combined-speed formula indicates that the vehicle was traveling approximately fifty-one miles per hour when it initially exited the east side of the roadway. The posted speed limit is thirty-five miles per hour. The initial loss of control was caused by Dawson's attempt to avoid striking a deer in the roadway rather than by vehicle speed.

[handwritten margin note: 51 mph when veered left to avoid deer]

The lack of a guardrail on the west side of the roadway in an area with a steep drop-off allowed the vehicle to exit the roadway and strike a utility pole. In addition, several trees—including the large tree struck by the right side of the vehicle—had been allowed to grow in the clear zone within thirty inches of the edge of pavement. This clearly created a hazard in that any vehicle exiting the roadway in this area would be directed down the grade and unable to avoid striking the tree. Within three weeks of the collision, the guard rail had been extended to protect this area and the trees in the clear zone were cut down.

Summary of Conclusions

In summary, based on what is known at this time, I am of the opinion that:

- Dawson was traveling northbound on Canyon Road, negotiating a curve toward the left and unexpectedly observed a deer in the roadway.

- Dawson steered to the right to avoid striking the deer, and the right tires of the vehicle drove off the right (east) edge of pavement.

- The angle at which the rutting departs from the edge of pavement is consistent with being preceded by an evasive maneuver.

- Dawson attempted to re-enter the roadway and overcorrected, causing the vehicle to rotate counterclockwise and exit the west edge of pavement in an area unprotected by a guard rail at that time.

- The front of the vehicle struck a utility pole, and the right, front door struck a large tree, which was approximately thirty inches from the edge of pavement.

- The vehicle was traveling approximately fifty-one miles per hour when it initially exited the east side of the roadway. The posted speed limit is thirty-five miles per hour.

- The initial loss of control was caused by Dawson's attempt to avoid striking a deer in the roadway rather than by vehicle speed.

- The lack of a guardrail on the west side of the roadway created a hazard in that a vehicle exiting the roadway in this area would be directed down the grade and unable to avoid striking the tree, which had been allowed to grow close to the edge of the pavement.

- Within three weeks of the collision, the guardrail had been extended to protect this area and the trees alongside the road were cut down.

We appreciate your confidence in our professional services.

Sincerely,

EXPERT ACCIDENT RECONSTRUCTION, INC.

Leslie Roman, PE, ACTAR

Senior Forensic Engineer

Attachments

Exhibit 12

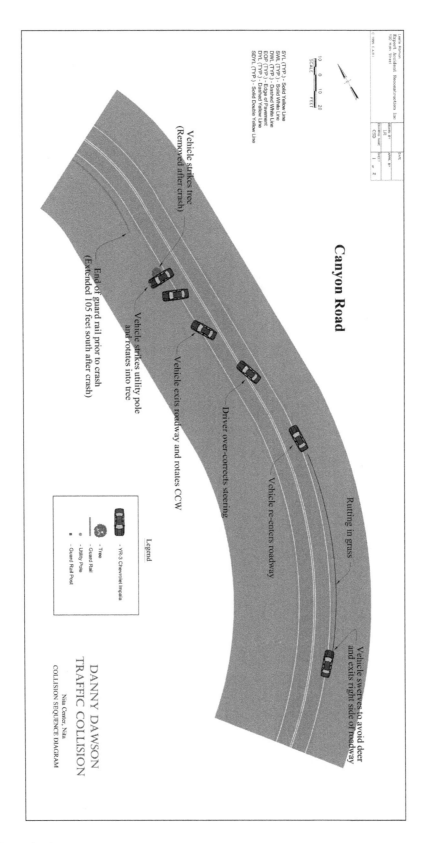

Canyon Road

Vehicle strikes tree
(Removed after crash)

End of guard rail prior to crash
(Extended 105 feet south after crash)

Vehicle strikes utility pole
and rotates into tree

Vehicle exits roadway and rotates CCW

Driver over-corrects steering

Vehicle re-enters roadway

Rutting in grass

Vehicle swerves to avoid deer
and exits right side of roadway

SYL (TYP.) - Solid Yellow Line
SWL (TYP.) - Solid White Line
DWL (TYP.) - Dashed White Line
EOP (TYP.) - Edge of Pavement
DYL (TYP.) - Dashed Yellow Line
SDYL (TYP.) - Solid Double Yellow Line

SCALE
10   0   10   20
FEET

Legend

- YFR-3 Chevrolet Impala
- Tree
- Guard Rail
- Utility Pole
- Guard Rail Post

DANNY DAWSON
TRAFFIC COLLISION

Nita Center, Nita
COLLISION SEQUENCE DIAGRAM

Exhibit 13

Photograph 0001: Vehicle at final rest. Rear tires remain on paved surface. Front of vehicle at rest against utility pole and right side of vehicle in contact with a tree (police photo).

EARI Project 10.20A

Exhibit 13

Photograph 0002: Rear tires of vehicle remain on the white (fog) line (police photo).

EARI Project 10.20A

Exhibit 13

Photograph 0003: Front of vehicle extends off pavement into ditch with the front bumper against a utility pole (police photo).

EARI Project 10.20A

Exhibit 13

Photograph 0004: Front of vehicle contacted utility pole (police photo).

EARI Project 10.20A

Exhibit 13

Photograph 0005: Right rear tire at final rest on the white (fog) line (police photo).

EARI Project 10.20A

Exhibit 13

Photograph 0006: Right front tire in ditch at final rest (police photo).

EARI Project 10.20A

Exhibit 13

Photograph 0007: Front bumper structure deformed by contact with utility pole (police photo).

EARI Project 10.20A

Exhibit 13

Photograph 0008: Deformation evident at right front door due to contact with tree.

EARI Project 10.20A

Exhibit 13

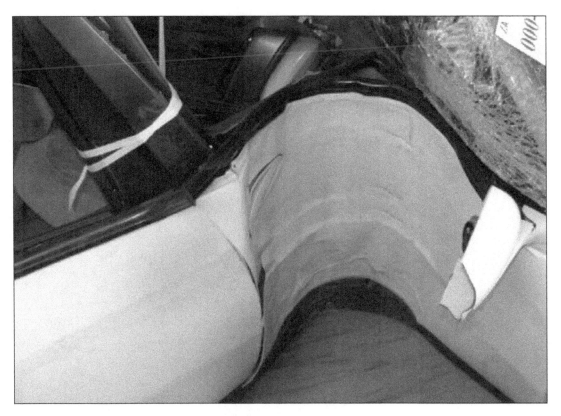

Photograph 0009: Deformed right front door due to contact with tree.

EARI Project 10.20A

Exhibit 13

Photograph 0010: Northbound Canyon Road approximately 1 mile south of crash site. Deer crossing sign is visible on right side of road.

EARI Project 10.20A

Exhibit 13

Photograph 0011: Northbound Canyon Road. Guard rail extended approximately 105 feet south after collision.

EARI Project 10.20A

Exhibit 13

Photograph 0012: Northbound Canyon Road. Utility pole remains on the left side of the roadway. New section of guard rail is on the left side of the roadway. No tiremarks are visible on the roadway.

EARI Project 10.20A

Exhibit 13

Photograph 0013: Several trees alongside the road in the area of the collision were cut down after the incident.

EARI Project 10.20A

Exhibit 13

Photograph 0014: Tree struck by right side of vehicle was approximately 39 inches in diameter at the base. Tree was cut down after the collision.

EARI Project 10.20A

Exhibit 13

Photograph 0015: View of the new section of guard rail and the slope of terrain away from the roadway.

EARI Project 10.20A

Exhibit 14

Vehicle Accident Reconstruction
A Primer
By Michael Windsor & Danielle Strasberg

Energy Speed Equivalent

Conservation of energy can be used to calculate the speed at which a vehicle strikes an immovable object. A vehicle which is moving has a certain amount of Kinetic Energy. A higher speed means that more energy is available to deform the vehicle when it strikes an object.

Consider the simple case of a vehicle striking a concrete bridge abutment head-on, crushing the front of the vehicle rearward by twenty-four inches (two feet) across the entire width of the vehicle. In this case, the full width of the front bumper would be pushed rearward twenty-four inches due to the collision. A formula developed empirically to calculate speed at the point of impact is:

V = Square root of (30 × D × CF) **Equation 1**

V = the speed (in mph) equivalent of the energy required to crush a vehicle

D = the maximum crush depth, measured in FEET

CF = the Crush Factor

   21 for frontal impacts

   27 for side impacts

   17 to 27 for rear impacts

In our case above, Equation 1 becomes:

V = Square Root (30 × 2 × 21)

V = Square Root (1260)

V = 35.5 mph

The V that has been calculated is equivalent speed lost due to the crushing of the vehicle. If this is only one part of the collision under study, the calculated V must be used in the "Combined Speed Formula."

NOTE: If the vehicle strikes a narrow object (for example, less than two feet in diameter), an adjustment must be made. In this case, the crush is not across the full width of the vehicle, but is concentrated in an area approximately two feet wide. Equation 1 then becomes:

V = Square Root of (30 × D × CF × 0.6) **Equation 2**

Combined Speed Formula

It is not uncommon for a single vehicle to travel through several phases or segments of a collision. For example, a vehicle may travel on the grass for fifty feet, then slide sideways on asphalt for another 100 feet before striking an immovable object at forty mph. The speed loss for each section must be calculated, and then the speeds are combined using the combined speed formula.

First, the speed loss of each section is calculated:

S = Square Root of (30 × D × f)   **Equation 3**

Where

        S = the speed loss in mph during that section

        D = the distance traveled in that particular section, in FEET

        F = the drag factor

Once the speed loss of each section is known, they are used to calculate the speed at the beginning of the first segment with the Combined Speed Formula below:

S = Square Root of ($S1^2$ + $S2^2$ + $S3^2$. . . .)   **Equation 4**

It is NOT correct simply to add the speed loss during each segment to calculate the total speed loss. Please note the superscript '2,' indicating that the value is to be squared.

Using our example above, there are three distinct segments to be analyzed. The final segment is the vehicle striking the immovable object. It has already been determined by other means that the vehicle was traveling forty mph when it hit the object, so the speed loss of Segment 3 is already known.

        S_3 = 40 mph

During Segment 2, the vehicle traveled 100 feet on asphalt on the road. Assuming a drag factor of 0.5, the speed loss during this segment (using Equation 3) is:

        S_2 = Square Root of (30 × D × f)

        S_2 = Square Root of (30 × 100 × 0.5)

        S_2 = Square Root of (1500)

        S_2 = 38.7 mph

During Segment 1, the vehicle traveled on a grass shoulder for fifty feet. Assuming a drag factor of 0.2, the speed loss during this segment (again, using Equation 3) is:

        S_1 = Square Root of (30 × D × f)

S_1 = Square Root of $(30 \times 50 \times 0.2)$

S_1 = Square Root of (300)

S_1 = 17.3 mph

To determine the speed of the vehicle at the beginning of Segment 1, where the car initially left the road, use Equation 4 above. For our example:

S = Square Root of $(S1^2 + S2^2 + S3^2)$

S = Square Root of $(17.3^2 + 38.7^2 + 40^2)$

S = Square Root of $(299 + 1498 + 1600)$

S = Square Root of (3397)

S = 58 mph

Drag Factors

The drag factor can be compared to the aggregate friction between all four tires and the roadway. The drag factor is used in calculating a vehicle's speed loss during a segment of a collision, whether it is due to braking, a slide, or deceleration due to the driver taking his foot off the accelerator. There are several ways to determine the drag factor. Two common methods are outlined below.

Use of Tables to Determine Drag Factor

Published tables can be used to determine the drag factor. For example, on a level roadway the following drag factors may apply:

Dry asphalt surface with locked brakes	0.7
Dry Asphalt surface—vehicle rotates 90 degrees (no braking)	0.5
Dry road—coasting (foot off brake)	0.1 to 0.2
Coasting on soft shoulder (foot off brake)	0.2 to 0.4
Locked brakes on wet roadway	0.2 to 0.5*
*Extremely dependent upon roadway conditions	
Vehicle rotates 90 degrees on wet roadway (no braking)	0.1 to 0.4*
*Extremely dependent upon roadway conditions	

[handwritten: There are our situations, & depends largely on road conditions]

Use of Drag Sled to Determine Drag Factor

A drag sled is constructed of a weighted section of tire with a sliding pull scale. The tire is dragged on the roadway. By making a comparison of the weight on the tire to the force required to pull the tire, the maximum drag factor of a roadway can be calculated.

There is much debate within the Vehicle Accident Reconstruction community as to the validity of results calculated with a drag sled. One of the primary concerns is that the drag sled is extremely sensitive to operator error; if the drag sled is not pulled exactly parallel to the road, an error (often a large one) will be induced.

A second major complaint about using the drag sled is more fundamental. Testing has not proven or disproven whether an old segment of tire filled with weight (concrete) pulled at a walking speed properly simulates an inflated tire supporting a 3,000-pound automobile traveling at highway speeds. Duplicating the exact weather conditions for a drag sled test, especially wet roadways, can also be problematic. Testing to compare the results of drag sleds to other methods has been inconclusive. Nonetheless, some experts continue to use the devices.

1) highly susceptible to human error

2) as a practice, highly disputed practice/technique b/c question whether it fundamentally simulates can

3) duplicating wet roadway conditions also very difficult

inconclusive whether this testing is as good as other methods or even addresses the concerns trying to be addressed

Exhibit 15

WELCOME TO CHUGGIE'S!!!!

For a complete list of all liquor available, ask your server

Specialty Shots

$5.00

Chuggie Bomb — Our Signature Drink! Herbal Liqueur, Energy Drink

Lemon Drop — Vodka, Lemon Juice, sugar cube

Purple Haze — Vodka, Blue Curaçao, Cranberry Juice

Kamikaze — Vodka, Triple Sec, Lime Juice

Woo — Vodka, Peach Schnapps, Cranberry Juice

Watermelon — Vodka, Melon Liquor, Cranberry Juice, Orange Juice

Blue Lagoon — Blue Curaçao, Vodka, Triple Sec, Lime Juice

Blue Slammer — Blue Curaçao, Sambuca, Vodka, Lemon Juice

Caribou Lou — Dark Rum, Coconut Rum, Pineapple Juice

Cherry Bomb — Cherry-Flavored Vodka, Energy Drink, Grenadine

Snake Bite — Bourbon, Tequila

Mixed Drinks

House $3.00 – Top Shelf $6.00

If You Don't See It Here, Ask

We Will Mix Anything!

Screwdriver — Vodka, Orange Juice

Jack & Ginger — Whiskey, Ginger Ale

Margarita — Tequila, Triple Sec, Lime Juice

Cosmo — Vodka, Triple Sec, Lime Juice, Cranberry Juice

Tequila Sunrise — Tequila, Orange Juice, Grenadine

Special Iced Teas

$6.00

Long Island — Gin, Vodka, Rum, Triple Sec, Cola

Miami — Gin, Vodka, Rum, Triple Sec, Pineapple Juice

Seaside — Gin, Vodka, Rum, Triple Sec, Cranberry Juice

Beers on Tap

$3.50

We regret to inform you that we no longer serve non-alcoholic beer

House Brews (5.5% Alcohol per Volume to 6.7% Alcohol per Volume)

    IPA, Brown, Stout

Wines

Prices are by the glass; we do not sell wines by the bottle

Horse's Head Sauvignon Blanc	$4.00
Horse's Head Merlot	$4.00
Low Plateau Pinot Grigio	$6.00
Low Plateau Merlot	$6.00

AFFIDAVIT OF LONDON BENNETT

After being duly sworn upon oath, London Bennett hereby deposes and states as follows.

1 My name is London Bennett. I have lived for many years in Nita Center, Nita. I live at 5234
2 Canyon Road. The Bennetts are the only ones who have ever occupied that ten-acre stretch
3 of land. My family is all gone now, but my dog, Peaches, and I keep a good eye on the place.
4 My family made a lot of money in the film industry, and since I'm the only one still living, I get
5 to live a pretty comfortable and charmed life. I have a little garden, and I love to sit on my porch
6 and paint. Canyon Road is pretty quiet, and my house is the only one that overlooks the road.
7 There are sometimes some wild animals that sniff around, but Peaches is pretty good at scaring
8 them off, and what her bark doesn't scare away, my shotgun turns into a pretty tasty dinner.
9
10 Canyon Road has a really nice view, and it is great for nature watching, but it is also really
11 dangerous. There isn't a lot of traffic on the road, so people are always taking the curves a
12 little too quickly. I can't tell you how many times I've seen people nearly fly right over the
13 cliff when the road drops down to two lanes. I have seen a few fender-benders and too many
14 near-misses to count, and I'm sad to say that I have seen another accident prior to this one
15 in which two kids were killed. The speed limit on that stretch of road is thirty-five miles per
16 hour, but I have tried many times to get the city to drop it down to twenty-five. Two years ago,
17 I went to a City Council meeting with a fifty-signature petition in hand to try to get the city to
18 change the speed limit and to extend the existing guardrails further down the road. They didn't
19 listen, though. Apparently, a couple of dead kids did not convince anyone that the road was
20 dangerous. The City Council chose to listen to the District Attorney, Ms. Sullivan, instead of
21 me. Ms. Sullivan argued that the road wasn't dangerous, drunk drivers were dangerous, and
22 all the fatal accidents had involved drinking and driving. People do use Canyon Road a lot late
23 at night after the bars in Nita Center shut down. So instead of changing the speed limit, the
24 City just ordered more cops to patrol the road in order to catch drunk drivers. I still see people
25 drive through too fast, though, and more cops don't make the road any less dangerous. I hope
26 this case and the death of Ms. Sullivan's own kid will be enough to wake people up and get the
27 speed limit changed. They have at least extended the guard rail so people will stop hitting trees
28 every time they swerve to avoid an animal. I guess that's better than nothing.
29
30 I was sitting on my front porch painting the storm on the Friday night Vanessa Sullivan died,
31 September 24, YR-2. I guess it was really Saturday morning when the accident happened.
32 I hadn't planned on being outside so late, but I was working on this painting that required the
33 exact coloring of rain on a wet street, so I wanted to take advantage of the weather. The storm
34 was predicted to hit sometime after midnight (it had been on all the news stations that day),
35 and sure enough, around 11:45 p.m., it started to sprinkle. I got out my brushes and paints and
36 settled myself down for what I thought would be a nice evening. I had just started painting
37 when I saw the NCPD car make its usual pass down the road heading into town. I figured it
38 was Officer Foster planning to set up the regular weekend post to watch cars as the late-night
39 crowd from town started to make their way back home. I didn't have a watch on me, but
40 I guess it was about midnight when I saw the officer drive past.

Handwritten margin notes: another fatal accident w/ kids / Road v. dangerous, people speed more / cops on Rd. / asked city to lower limit + didn't / DA fought it + now her kid died there too / feeling even worse, needs someone to blame

1   The rain was trickling down until a few minutes before the accident. I was sitting on my porch,
2   and the skies opened up and the rain started pouring down in sheets. It was like someone had
3   turned a million buckets of water over all at once. Right after that, I heard a siren in the dis-
4   tance. Peaches started barking like crazy. I don't know if it was the lightning, the thunder, or
5   an animal, but she was looking pretty intensely in the direction of the road. I looked up to see
6   if I needed to grab my shotgun, but instead of an animal, I saw a car careening down the road.
7   I tried to yell at them to slow down, but I don't think they could've heard me. The car was going
8   way too fast for the weather, probably at least twenty miles per hour or more above the posted
9   speed limit, but I wasn't clocking it. I've seen cars make it through going that quickly before,
10   but it seemed like a pretty dangerous decision to me. All of a sudden, the car jerked to the right
11   and then swerved back with a quick turn to the left, and next thing I knew, it was spinning
12   across the road and into a tree. The first thing I did was call the cops. I knew there was an officer
13   nearby, and I don't know why that cop didn't see or stop this car or what the cop was doing, but
14   I hoped someone would get to the road fast. I told the 911 operator my address and that I had
15   witnessed a crazy driver go flying off the road. I also told them that they are supposed to have
16   cops on the road to stop people from speeding and now there were probably even more people
17   dead because nobody would listen to me about adding the guardrail all the way down the curve.
18   The dispatcher said they would send someone out. When I hung up, I ran straight down to the
19   road to see if I could help.
20
21   From where I was sitting on my porch, about 100 feet from the road, I thought the car had just
22   hit a tree. The car actually crashed into a utility pole, too. I don't know how fast they were
23   going, but it looked like they were speeding pretty fast, and at that rate, hitting a pole and a tree,
24   I expected everyone in the car to be dead. I was relieved when I got to the car and noticed a
25   person wandering around in circles in the road muttering, "Oh my God! Oh my God!" over and
26   over again. I heard another person screaming inside the car. I was just glad people were alive.
27
28   I approached the person in the road first, and I learned the person's name was Danny Dawson.
29   Danny's forehead was bleeding a little, but other than that, Danny seemed to be OK. I asked
30   Danny if anyone else was in the car, and Danny said, "She's OK. She was just talking to her
31   dad." Danny seemed pretty shaken up, but he was not stumbling or slurring words or anything
32   when we spoke. I've seen plenty of drunken people before, and Danny didn't seem to be drunk,
33   just shaken up. I tried to tell Danny that thousands of people have had problems on that road
34   and if anyone was to blame, it was the City of Nita for allowing people to drive so fast on a dan-
35   gerous curve with no guardrail. At that point, Danny started rambling about "Jack and Ginger."
36   Danny seemed to be blaming "Jack and Ginger" and muttering over and over, "So stupid, why
37   did I let them talk me into driving when I knew I was tipsy?" I thought maybe Jack and Ginger
38   were the other people in the car, and I decided to go check on them.
39
40   As I made my way to the car, I could hear the police sirens in the background, and I saw
41   two people in the car. At first I thought maybe one of them was Jack or Ginger, but as I got
42   closer, I recognized Taylor Hopson in the backseat, slumped over. My heart dropped. I have
43   known Taylor since the Hopsons moved to Nita Center. Taylor's dad does extra work around
44   my house sometimes. At that point, I ran to check on Taylor and the other passenger, whom
45   I then knew was definitely Vanessa Sullivan, Taylor's best friend. Even though Danny claimed

scared kid in denial about tragic event

1   Vanessa was OK, when I got to the car, Vanessa definitely wasn't. She wasn't responding at all.
2   Taylor was starting to stir, but Vanessa's eyes were closed, and no matter what I did to shake
3   her, she wouldn't respond. I put my hand under her nose to see if I could feel air. I felt nothing,
4   and I knew Vanessa wasn't breathing. I yelled for Danny to come help, but Danny just said,
5   "No, Vanessa is fine. She has to be fine or my life is over." I wanted to do CPR, but I was not
6   sure how to get her out of her seatbelt or the car.
7   *← ugh this guy is such a dick*

8   That's when the police and the ambulance got to the scene. Officer Foster seemed to be in
9   charge, and after everything calmed down, Officer Foster asked me to step over and answer a
10 few questions. The officer asked me what I saw and whether I had spoken to any of the people
11 in the car. I told the officer everything I had observed and the things Danny told me when I got
12 to the scene. I remember Officer Foster asked me if I saw anything else on the road at the time   *seen*
13 of the accident, like a deer or another car. I told the officer that I see deer on the road pretty   *deer*
14 regularly (I have a collection of paintings entitled "Deer Eyes on a Dark Street"), but that I did   *frequently but looking*
15 not see any animals on the road that night, and I was looking pretty carefully after Peaches   *closely &*
16 started raising a fuss. I did mention that Peaches had run toward the road just before the acci-   *didn't see*
17 dent, but Peaches is only about twenty pounds, would never stray far from the porch on a rainy   *one*
18 night, and could never be confused with a deer. I then asked Officer Foster if Vanessa was
19 going to be OK, but Officer Foster would not respond. I found out the next day that Vanessa
20 had died. I felt so awful. It was the second worst accident I've seen, next to the high-school
21 kids that died a few years back. I hope the city learns a lesson and reduces the speed limit so
22 no more accidents happen.
23
24 Of the exhibits in this case, I am familiar with the following: Accident Photos 0010 through
25 0015, which were shown to me by attorneys in this case and which I agree are accurate depic-
26 tions of images of Canyon Road and the crash scene contained therein. I am not familiar with
27 any other exhibits or any affidavits other than my own.

I hereby attest to having read the above statement and swear or affirm it to be my own. I also
swear or affirm to the truthfulness of its content. Before giving this statement, I was told it
should contain everything I knew that might be relevant to my testimony, and I followed those
instructions. I also understand that I can and must update this affidavit if anything new occurs
to me until the moment before I testify in this case.

                                    /s/ LB
                                    London Bennett

Subscribed and sworn before on this, the 3rd day of October, YR-2.

                                    /s/ SS
                                    Sarah Shelton, Notary Public

AFFIDAVIT OF DANNY DAWSON

After being duly sworn upon oath, Danny Dawson hereby deposes and states as follows.

1　My name is Danny Dawson. I am currently a senior at Calkins College in East Hill, Nita.
2　I'm majoring in urban studies, and linguistics is my minor—not a typical combination, but
3　I find both subjects fascinating. It's pretty easy to pick an interesting major when you can do
4　anything you want. The pre-law advisor told me that I could pick any major I wanted—you
5　see, I've been set on heading to Calkins Law since I was in the second grade and starred as
6　an attorney in my class's mock trial of *The Three Little Pigs v. the Big Bad Wolf*. All I had
7　to do was keep a high GPA and turn in a solid LSAT performance. And I was halfway there;
8　the A− I picked up in sociolinguistic theory is the only thing that's kept me from a 4.0.
9
10　Before going off to college, I spent my high-school years in the northern suburbs of Nita
11　Center. After my senior year of high school, I swore I would never go anywhere near Nita Cen-
12　ter again. I was a finalist for a scholarship to Pennington University, but everything changed
13　on senior prom night. My friends and I had used our fake IDs to get into Chuggie's that night
14　after leaving the dance. I was on my way home when a police officer pulled me over. Getting
15　pulled over was no surprise in Nita Center; the local police treat "driving while a teenager" like
16　it's a felony. That night, the officer made me do all sorts of tests and then booked me for a DUI.
17　Maybe I'd had a couple of beers at the bar, but that was way earlier in the evening. There's no
18　chance that alcohol was still in my system. Since I was eighteen and did not want the charge
19　on my record forever, I pleaded the charge down to reckless driving and went through a pre-
20　trial diversion program. My arrest record was wiped clean after I did 100 hours of community
21　service and wore an ankle bracelet that ensured I did not go into any twenty-one-and-over bars
22　for a year. Unfortunately for me, Pennington University must have gotten wind of the charges,
23　and I didn't get the scholarship. Goodbye elite university, hello Calkins College.
24
25　I was pretty unhappy about having to stay in Nita then, but I tried to make the best of it. I focused
26　my efforts on academics and making Calkins a better place, and I have really came to love it
27　there. I was vice-president of student government my junior year and did some writing for the
28　newspaper. We also have the best basketball team around, and I love to camp out with friends
29　and go crazy at the games. I also had scheduled a meeting for the first week of October YR-2
30　with a major donor to pitch a great idea for a new community-service organization. But, as you
31　probably know, my life is kind of on hold after what happened to Vanessa last September. I'm
32　taking some time off from school and gathering my thoughts. I feel like I'm constantly on trial,
33　whether it's part of a court proceeding or in the media. I guess that's what happens when you're
34　behind the wheel the night the daughter of the district attorney tragically loses her life.
35
36　Vanessa Sullivan and I met in the fall of our sophomore year. The two of us shared a major, and
37　we were taking an introductory urban studies class together. I made a point to talk to her since
38　I knew that her mom was one of the state's most successful attorneys. The cases Vanessa's
39　mom prosecuted were always in the headlines. The more I chatted with Vanessa, the more
40　I realized that she was pretty cool in her own right. We didn't really run in the same circles,

1   but we kept ending up in the same classes. I'd say that I was in a half-dozen study groups with

2   Vanessa, and we had coffee a few times. She would always listen when I would talk about using

3   the law as a way to help stabilize urban areas and turn them around. Most of my friends' eyes

4   just kind of glazed over. I'd call Vanessa a pretty solid friend, but she's not somebody I called

5   over the summer or anything.

6

7   In early September, I arrived a few minutes early to my senior seminar course for my major

8   when I overheard Vanessa on the phone. She was talking about going to Nita Center the week-

9   end of the September 24 for her birthday. I could barely believe it when she said that she was

10   going to Chuggie's to watch the band Chatterbox that Friday night. I had hung out at Chuggie's

11   just about every night when I had an internship in Nita Center the previous summer. They have

12   the best live music in town, and Chatterbox is my favorite band ever! Naturally, I struck up a

13   conversation with Vanessa about her plans, and she told me that she was headed back to town for

14   her twenty-first birthday. We talked a little more, and I found out that she lived in the town next

15   to mine. It's a couple of hours from East Hill to Nita Center, but I was willing to make the trip

16   for Chatterbox. I hinted as much, complained about not having a car on campus, and picked up

17   an offer from Vanessa to ride to town with her. She did say that I might have to be the designated

18   driver on the night of the concert. That was a small price to pay for such an awesome event, and

19   I'm a veteran when it comes to playing it safe, but still having a few drinks and a good time.

20

21   Neither of us had Friday classes, so we left school after our last class on the September 23 and

22   had an uneventful drive to Nita Center. I was pretty shocked to see that Vanessa had a radar

23   detector in her car with Ms. Sullivan being a prosecutor; Vanessa told me that it should be

24   our little secret. Vanessa dropped me off at my aunt's house, and I told her that I'd meet her

25   at Chuggie's the next night. I was already going to be in Nita Center the next afternoon for an

26   interview I'd lined up once I knew I was coming into town. It made sense that I would just have

27   my aunt drop me off for my interview downtown, and I figured I'd just meet up with Vanessa

28   and Taylor afterwards. Taylor does not go to school with us, but Vanessa told me that Taylor

29   was also planning to apply to Calkins Law, so I figured that Taylor would be pretty cool to meet.

30

31   My aunt drove me in to Nita Center on Friday for a lunch interview having to do with a summer

32   internship. The interview was right next door to Chuggie's, which is a pretty chill place dur-

33   ing the day. I decided to head on over to Chuggie's at 2:00 p.m. I was happy to see that Jordan

34   James was around for the afternoon. Jordan is a good buddy of mine, and I told Jordan that

35   this would be a good day to make them strong and keep them coming; the interview didn't go

36   that well, and I was hoping to forget it. Of course, I always told Jordan to make them strong,

37   and I don't think I actually got any stronger drinks than normal. That's when Jordan told me

38   that the opening act for Chatterbox was actually the bartender. It took me a minute to realize

39   what Jordan meant, but when I did, I gave Jordan a high-five and told Jordan to let me buy the

40   bartender a shot to celebrate. Jordan told me there was no need to buy anything and poured us

41   each a shot of something. We tipped the drinks back in honor of Jordan's biggest gig to date.

42

43   A bit later that afternoon, Sam Lyons came into the bar and asked if I already had a taxi ride

44   scheduled. I told Lyons that I was meeting two friends later in the day and that I was pretty sure

45   that one of them was going to be driving us home that night. I wasn't sure though, so I think

[handwritten in left margin near lines 32–33: got to bar @ 2pm]

[handwritten top margin: demonstrating exp. familiarity w/ ale & serious trusted man to help w/ limits]

[handwritten: 4 drinks + 1 shot from 2–7 pm   5 ham 2–7]

1 I only had three whiskey-and-ginger-ales and one beer while I sat around and read for the
2 most of the afternoon. I felt pretty confident that I'd make good decisions with Jordan around;
3 Jordan really knows my limits. Also, there was a pocket breathalyzer around the bar the entire
4 summer before that I used to develop a pretty good sense of my tolerance. I knew that if
5 I stayed at a drink an hour or lower that I'd be golden.
6
7 I had just finished my novel around 7:00 p.m. when Vanessa and Taylor showed up. I think
8 I vaguely recognized Taylor, but I'm not sure. When they arrived, I left the bar area and fol- *[1 whiskey]*
9 lowed them to a table closer to the stage. Pat Lawrence, the server in that section, came to take
10 our order. I had a whiskey on the rocks with dinner and bought shots for Taylor and Vanessa.
11 It was a night of celebration, and it was still early in the evening, so I figured it was no big
12 deal to drink a bit. I think I heard Taylor say something about being the designated driver, so
13 I wasn't really that worried. I don't remember exactly what I ate for dinner, but I know I had
14 a ton of cheese fries.
15
16 After dinner, I went to the bar and chatted with Jordan for a while. I had enjoyed chatting *[1 shot]*
17 with Vanessa and Taylor, and Taylor seemed pretty psyched about being possible law-school *[1 beer]*
18 classmates, but I figured the two of them would want to catch up on old times, and I wanted *[by 9.30]*
19 to compliment Jordan on a great job on the opening set. As soon as I got to the bar, Jordan and
20 I had a shot and chased it with a beer. I still wasn't too worried about the drinking because it
21 did not look like I was driving, and the night was still young; it could not have been later than
22 9:30 at that point.
23
24 A little after 10:00 p.m., I made my way back over to Taylor and Vanessa's table to see if *[½ drink]*
25 we could move a little closer to where Chatterbox was going to perform. The two of them
26 agreed, and we started to chat a bit more. Somebody sent a drink over for Vanessa since she
27 was the birthday girl, but she did not seem interested in drinking it. Taylor and I both had a sip
28 to finish it. Pat came by with drinks on the house for my companions and me. I think Jordan *[1 drink]*
29 sent them over. My whiskey-and-ginger-ale was delicious, and I was sipping away on it when
30 Chatterbox took the stage. I was psyched, and I think I spilled half of my drink from jumping
31 up and down in excitement. Chatterbox was better than ever before. Everyone looking at me
32 must have thought that I was dancing like I was drunk. I was maybe a little tipsy, but I am
33 really just a terrible dancer. I am so uncoordinated; you can just ask Jordan. I try to throw darts
34 every time I am at the bar, and Jordan usually takes them away when the place gets crowded
35 because my aim is terrible even when I am sober. Fortunately, I didn't try to throw any darts
36 that night. The bar was way too crowded for that.
37
38 At the end of the first set, I talked my way backstage to try to meet the band, which I had seen
39 at Chuggie's a few times before. The band manager wouldn't let me through until I told her it *[1 drink]*
40 was Vanessa's birthday. When I pointed to Vanessa and Taylor, the manager smiled and called *[by]*
41 the band over, and before I knew it, we had drinks in our hands to celebrate the awesomeness
42 of the night. We toasted to great Friday nights, and one of the band members made a comment *[mid.]*
43 about Saturday mornings, so it must have been after midnight. I wasn't slurring or anything
44 at all, and I just loved it that I was chatting with such a great musician. I thought Vanessa
45 and Taylor would be pretty impressed that I had gotten us in with the band, so I called them

1   over to chat with Chatterbox, too. It turns out Vanessa and Taylor knew the lead singer from
2   high school and had met the whole band before, which is why the band manager smiled at me.
3   Taylor got a good laugh out of making me feel silly, but nothing was going to kill my buzz on
4   such a good night.
5
6   I was feeling pretty good at this point, so instead of exiting the backstage area toward the bar,
7   I found myself walking onto the stage. Well, when in Rome. . . . I grabbed a guitar and started
8   strumming. Everybody was cheering like crazy for me. There's no way I could have played so
9   well if I was drunk at the time; I'm bad enough when I'm sober. Some big guy—I guess it was
10   a roadie or a bouncer or something—grabbed hold of me, but Vanessa was behind him and told
11   him to lay off and apologized for me. I don't know why, the crowd loved it. The crowd cheered
12   again for me as the guy helped me get down from the stage. It was awesome.
13
14   Chatterbox was back on stage, and time was just flying because we were having so much fun.
15   Next thing I knew, I looked up and Taylor was actually on the stage singing a song with the
16   band! I'm not sure if Taylor was invited, but I was impressed. I also realized that Taylor was
17   pretty drunk and that I was the most likely candidate to drive. About that time, Pat walked over
18   to see how I was doing. I ordered a tequila sunrise because I really wanted this night to last
19   until morning, so I had the sunrise on my mind. Pat asked me if I needed help booking a cab,
20   and I told Pat that I was driving home. Pat told me to stop kidding and said that Jordan had
21   really been pouring my drinks strong and that I should take a taxi. I was a little tipsy still, but
22   the tequila sunrise was going to be my last drink. I knew I would be fine when things closed
23   down in an hour. I went ahead and asked Pat to get me some sodas and to keep them coming
24   after I finished the tequila sunrise. It was time for me to sober up, but I also needed the caffeine.
25
26   I was double-fisting some soda trying to stay awake when I made it back over to Vanessa and
27   Taylor. Taylor was talking about how awesome it was to sing on stage, and I just wished it
28   could've been me. Taylor and Vanessa were pretty drunk at that point, and I knew we would
29   need to leave soon. When Chatterbox was done, Jordan came over and saw if we wanted to do
30   another shot to celebrate a great night. We said yes, but I whispered to Pat to bring me water
31   instead of liquor. I figured everyone was too drunk to notice. I think Pat might have messed that
32   one up because Vanessa said something about water, and I felt a little burn in my shot, but I was
33   totally sober by that point. I certainly was no more than tipsy. I'd done most of my drinking
34   during the first part of the night, and I knew I was way under the legal limit. No chance I'd let
35   a DUI keep me out of Calkins Law.
36
37   As we left Chuggie's, I saw Sam Lyons parked in the usual spot outside the bar. I'd seen Lyons
38   at the bar that night hanging around and looking for a good customer. Lyons was my regular
39   taxi driver over the summer, and Lyons has seen me pretty wasted. I told Lyons I was doing
40   just fine, and Lyons told me to drive safely. I know Lyons would have stopped me if there was
41   a problem. Also, Lyons was in the bar and probably saw how responsible I had been. I would
42   have drunk way, way more if I were going to take a cab home.
43
44   Taylor was pretty wasted when we got to the car and started complaining about how I should
45   not be driving in the rainstorm and how I had already made us stay out too late. I was pretty

Handwritten margin notes: I drunk; I was shot Thought he was under legal limit; I hate this guy; blaming everyone else; Lyons would have stopped me

1   unhappy with Taylor since I think Taylor was supposed to be the designated driver. Taylor
2   started telling me how Vanessa and Taylor promised Vanessa's mom they would be home by
3   1:00 a.m., that it was already 12:45 a.m., and that the drive would take twenty minutes. I said
4   that I could do it in ten. Taylor told me there was no way I could make that happen with all of
5   the cops on the road. Not one to back down from a challenge, I remembered the radar detector
6   in Vanessa's car, pulled it out of the glove compartment, turned it on, and took off. I figured
7   nobody would pull me over for having an illegal radar detector at that time of night, and I was
8   going to make it to Vanessa's house in ten minutes. I knew from being around the Nita Center
9   bar crowd over the summer that Canyon Road is the most popular route to take if you are
10 trying to avoid cops. I remember Lyons warning me about the road—curves, deer, no lights,
11 more cops than there used to be. I think Sam was just looking to maintain a regular fare. Either
12 way, it wasn't like I was trying to avoid a DUI. Even if I got pulled over, I figured Vanessa's
13 mom could take care of a little speeding ticket.   *This guy is repugnant*
14
15 When we left Chuggie's it had already started raining, and I hoped the rain wouldn't get any
16 worse while I was driving Vanessa and Taylor home. Vanessa and Taylor asked a few more
17 times if I was good enough to drive, and they kept saying it looked like I was swerving a bit,
18 but I chalked that up to their inebriation. They probably couldn't see straight, and I was trying
19 to live up to my promise to get there on time. I felt confident about speeding; the roads are
20 fairly familiar to me, and I figured if there were any cops, they wouldn't pull anyone over
21 so they wouldn't have to get out of their car and get soaked. Then the radar detector lit up,
22 and Taylor got worried and started complaining, but I slowed down in plenty of time. Taylor
23 started talking about how scared Taylor was, and I was a little worried, too. The police sure
24 are blinded by the need to blame around here. Instead of showing fear, as soon as the police
25 car was out of view, I sped up and started taking the curves a little more quickly. It was no big
26 deal, though. I've driven faster on that road before.
27
28 We couldn't have been more than a couple miles from Vanessa's house when we got to the big
29 curve on Canyon Road. Taylor was still being pretty loud in the back seat, and I could not wait
30 to get Taylor out of the car. I knew this part of the road was especially dangerous because a few
31 people had run off the road and hit the unguarded trees before. Vanessa was also worried about
32 me going too fast, so she said she would just call her dad and tell him we were almost there, but   *Taylor a distracting passenger*
33 the rain was going to make us a few minutes late. The whole time Vanessa was trying to talk
34 to her parents, Taylor would not shut up and kept making the radio louder. The radio, Taylor's   *both girls very drunk*
35 yammering, and the ridiculously loud music were really fraying my nerves. When I got close
36 to the big curve, I saw that the front-porch light was on at a house to my left, which seemed
37 odd at that time of night. Vanessa started yelling at me about something, but I wasn't sure what
38 because I couldn't hear her over all the noise in the car. My eyes were back on the road a few
39 seconds later when I saw something coming at us. I'm pretty sure it was a deer or something;   *saw something what he thought was a deer*
40 there are a lot of them on those back roads, but by this point the rain was coming down in
41 sheets, and it was hard to see. Whatever it was, it wasn't actually on my side of the road, but it
42 had to be moving toward my lane. I had to make a split-second decision. I steered the car to the
43 right a little harder than I should have, and I started to go down the embankment on the outside
44 of the curve. I tried to pull us back onto the road and lost control. The car went across both
45 lanes of traffic, and before I knew what was happening, the car hit a tree or a pole or something.

1 I was panicking. Taylor had stopped talking and just seemed to be sitting in the back seat in
2 shock. I tried to talk to Vanessa, but she was not responding at all. I remembered the front-porch
3 light and started trying to run toward it calling for help. I was met by a person I now know as
4 London Bennett. Bennett told me that Bennett saw everything from the front porch and had
5 already called 911. I told Bennett that I felt so bad about what happened and that I'd never be
6 able to be seen in Nita Center again if anything bad happened to Vanessa or Taylor. Before
7 I could launch into my tale of woe, I realized that Bennett was over at the car screaming that
8 Vanessa was not breathing. When I ran over, Taylor asked for my help to get out of the car, which
9 was crushed like a soda can. I don't know anything about rescue work, but I helped Taylor out of
10 the car. I was so worried about Vanessa and thought something terrible might happen.
11

12 Unfortunately, I was right. Vanessa didn't make it to the ambulance. Nothing could be done to
13 save her. The next thing I knew, Ms. Sullivan was there screaming at me about how she was
14 going to do everything in her power to put me in jail for life for what I did to her daughter. I told
15 her that I was sorry and that it was all my fault. I wanted to tell her that I wished I had taken
16 my chances with hitting the deer or whatever was in the road. Before I could say a word, she
17 was demanding that the police get my confession and confirm that my drunk driving caused
18 her daughter's death. I swore that I was fine, but no one was listening. The police made me do
19 all sorts of silly tests, and Ms. Sullivan kept going on about how she saw me fail every one of
20 them. I think I did just fine, but I have no idea. I did not give the police any statements that night
21 beyond whatever small talk I had with the officer that was first at the scene.

23 After seeing Ms. Sullivan, I knew that nothing good would come of it. I was right. The officer
24 at the scene threw me in the back of the police car, and the next thing I knew, I was at the police
25 station being booked on a bogus murder charge. My mind was reeling at that point. The two
26 officers at the station grabbed me roughly and tossed me into a holding cell like a bag of pota-
27 toes. There was another person in the cell with me—Sandy something-or-other was the name.
28 Seems like Sandy was getting railroaded by the cops too, though we didn't get to talk much.
29 Our chat ended when one of the cops came down to talk to me about running more tests, and
30 Sandy was gone before I got back to the holding cell.
31

32 I have no idea when driving a little fast and swerving away from a deer in the road on a rainy
33 night became murder, but I may never get to go to law school to find out. I was keeping pretty
34 close track, and I don't think I had more than a drink an hour that night. Like I've said before,
35 I know that a drink an hour is perfectly fine for me—always has been and always will be unless
36 a vindictive, malicious prosecutor comes after me. I feel worse than anyone about Vanessa
37 Sullivan's death, but her mom doesn't need to ruin someone else's life because of the horrible
38 accident on the night of Vanessa's twenty-first birthday.
39

40 I went to Vanessa's funeral on September 29 to pay my respects to her and her family. I felt
41 awful about what had happened, even though it was an accident. I skipped the church service
42 and went to the gravesite, where I was going to try to talk to Mr. Sullivan afterward to tell him
43 how sorry I was for what had happened. Before I had been there for two minutes, Taylor made a
44 beeline for me and told me to leave. I was surprised because Taylor was in the car, and I figured
45 Taylor of all people had to know there was a deer in the road, too, but when I tried to explain

Handwritten margin notes:
DA threatened Danny
The DA was @ the scene commenting on the tests
already had clean + bias stance against drunk driving

1   that Taylor told me there wasn't and once again told me to go away. I don't know why Taylor
2   said that, but I try to give people the benefit of the doubt. Maybe Taylor was just too drunk to
3   remember what happened that night. Anyway, if anyone was making things at the funeral bad
4   for the family, it was Taylor, not me. But out of respect to Vanessa and her family and other
5   friends, I decided to leave quietly, and I haven't tried to contact her family since. I did go visit
6   her at the cemetery after to tell her how sorry I am, and I hope someday her family will also
7   forgive me.
8
9   Of the available exhibits in this case, I am familiar with the following: Bar Tab #1 of Danny
10   Dawson and Bar Tab #2 of Danny Dawson, which were signed by me on September 24 and 25,
11   YR-2; Bar Tab #3 of Vanessa Sullivan, which Vanessa signed in my presence on September 25,
12   YR-2; Accident Photos 0001 through 0015, which were shown to me by my attorneys and
13   which I agree are accurate depictions of images contained therein; the Breath Test Operator's
14   Report, which I reviewed and signed on the date indicated; and the Voicemail Message, which
15   was provided to me by my attorneys. I can confirm that the speaking voice on the Voicemail
16   Message belongs to Vanessa Sullivan and that the Voicemail Message is the recording of the
17   call made by Vanessa that I reference in this affidavit. I am also familiar with the Chuggie's
18   Drink Menu, and, except where specifically noted elsewhere in my affidavit, I have no reason
19   to believe that any of the drinks served at Chuggie's on September 24 or 25, YR-2, either
20   omitted a component listed or added a component not listed with the corresponding drink on
21   the drink menu. I am not familiar with any other exhibits or any affidavits other than my own.

I hereby attest to having read the above statement and swear or affirm it to be my own. I also swear or affirm to the truthfulness of its content. Before giving this statement, I was told it should contain everything I knew that might be relevant to my testimony, and I followed those instructions. I also understand that I can and must update this affidavit if anything new occurs to me until the moment before I testify in this case. I have also read the opinions rendered by the experts I have hired to show my innocence in this case. They have offered all of the opinions I have requested and disclosed, and my counsel ensures me that all available information relevant to the experts' opinions has been provided to them.

_____/s/ DND_____
Danny N. Dawson

Subscribed and sworn before me on this, the 1st day of October, YR-2.

_____/s/ SS_____
Sarah Shelton, Notary Public

AFFIDAVIT OF RYAN FOSTER

After being duly sworn upon oath, Ryan Foster hereby deposes and states as follows:

1　My name is Ryan Foster. I am a patrol officer for the Nita Center Police Department. I earned
2　my bachelor of science in civil engineering from the Georgia Institute of Technology, where
3　I graduated with highest honors and took several courses in the field of transportation plan-
4　ning and design. I became a certified professional engineer in YR-13. While I had several
5　job offers with top civil-engineering firms, I decided that I wanted to combine my engineer-
6　ing education with my interest in law enforcement. I applied for a job with the Nita Center
7　Police Department (NCPD) after graduation and have been there for over ten years. I took a
8　twenty-two-week course at the Nita State Police Academy, where I learned the fundamen-
9　tals of police work, criminal law, criminal procedure, and investigation techniques. I have
10　also taken several refresher seminar courses in road design and safety and serve on the city
11　council's transportation safety board.

12

13　As far as my experience goes, I wear two hats. I have been a patrol officer for my entire time
14　at the NCPD, but since late YR-8, I have also been a member of the NCPD's Fatal Crash Team
15　(FCT). As a member of the FCT, I investigate the cause of traffic accidents with a focus on
16　accident reconstruction. I received my certification from the Accreditation Commission for
17　Traffic Accident Reconstructionists in May of YR-8.

18

19　On the night of September 24, YR-2, I was working solo patrol because my partner Bud Baker
20　had come down with the "Friday night flu," which seems to be a recurring illness. I was work-
21　ing my usual patrol in the Canyon Road area that night, and I lucked into the 11:00 p.m. to
22　7:00 a.m. shift. It started drizzling around 11:30 p.m. that night, so I stopped driving around
23　and moved my car to the fork in the road where Canyon Road and Chambers Avenue split.
24　I wanted to be able to stop any reckless drivers coming from the city toward where I see so
25　many accidents on Canyon Road, up near my good friend London Bennett's house. For the
26　most part, it was a quiet night. I pulled a blue Honda over for doing seventy-five in a thirty-five
27　at about 11:45 p.m. The driver was old Norris Eren. He's a friend of my grandpa's from college,
28　and I don't think he should be out on the road at all, so I didn't give him any sort of a break.
29　Reckless driving is not a joke. I was back to the fork in the road by midnight. By 12:30 a.m.,
30　the rain started coming down hard enough that I turned my wipers on.

31

32　Right about 12:55 a.m., the skies opened up. The first few cars that passed by after the deluge
33　had started were using emergency flashers, and my radar showed that none of them were going
34　faster than thirty-five miles per hour. I saw a newer-model Chevrolet Impala, coming from
35　the city, approach the fork in the road, and I got a radar reading of fifty-four miles per hour. *54 mph*
36　My radar gun was calibrated before I went on duty that night, and I never have any problems *on chevy*
37　getting an accurate reading. As the car got closer, I noticed a few things. First, the license plate
38　on the front of the car said SULLY3, so I knew it belonged to the Sullivan family. I really *knew car was*
39　appreciate all of the work Ms. Sullivan does as a prosecutor. I also noticed the car swerve a *DA's*
40　little bit. If it were a clear night, I'd probably be pulling the car over to check for a DUI, but

would've pulled over
for DUI on clear nights

1   with the downpour I figured Vanessa was just having a hard time driving or hydroplaning a
2   little bit. I was thinking about following the car when I got a call on my radio that assistance
3   was needed on Chambers Avenue with a motor-vehicle stop. I radioed in my location, turned
4   on my lights, and headed that way. If I really thought the driver of SULLY3 should have been
5   off the road, then I would have taken care of that situation first.

6

7   Before I got to the Chambers Avenue location, another call came in over the radio. There
8   had been a one-car accident on Canyon Road right across from London Bennett's house.
9   Apparently, Bennett had called it in from home, and immediate assistance was needed. I was
10   specifically told to report to the scene because it sounded like a member of the FCT might be
11   needed. My heart sank. I knew I should have stopped that car. I took a left on Yarbough Drive
12   and cut over to the scene of the accident. The Impala was on the side of the road. The front of
13   the car had slammed into a utility pole, and the passenger side had hit a tree. I parked my car in
14   Bennett's driveway so I would not block the emergency vehicles on the way and hustled down
15   to the scene of the accident.

16

17   Bennett and the person I later learned to be Danny Dawson were near the automobile, but nei-
18   ther of them was in the car. I heard a scream for help. When I got to the car, I saw that Vanessa
19   Sullivan was in the front seat on the side of the car that had slammed against the tree. She was
20   still strapped into her seat belt, but she was not responding. The paramedics arrived at about
21   that time, and I directed them to Vanessa. Another person, who I later learned was Taylor
22   Hopson, was in the back seat of the car. Hopson appeared to be bleeding from the head, and
23   Hopson's hands were covered in blood. Hopson was just screaming and screaming. I could
24   not tell exactly what Hopson was saying; all I could really make out was, "Don't make me
25   kill Danny for killing my best friend! Hold on, Vanessa!" Hopson also screamed something
26   about not being able to see anything in the rain and how the city should have closed down
27   the road.

28

29   I thought Hopson might be in some trouble, but the EMTs were focused completely on Vanessa
30   at that point. I then noticed that Hopson somehow had managed to get out of the car and was
31   standing on one side of me, and Dawson was on the other. Dawson was apologizing for not
32   doing a better job of driving the car and kept blaming the rain. Dawson kept saying, "Vanessa
33   can't die because of me; she just can't!" Dawson said that Dawson really did not know what
34   happened out there on the road. Then Dawson muttered something about needing another drink,
35   and it hit me that maybe Dawson's speech was a little slurred. I hadn't really noticed it before,
36   but it made sense, especially given that Dawson had driven a car off the side of the road. I asked
37   Dawson if Dawson wanted the EMTs to see if Dawson was injured, but Dawson said no.

38

39   Before I could ask Dawson any more questions, Dawson walked away from me and was stand-
40   ing near Vanessa. I stepped aside for a second and called Avery Smith, who handles Intoxilyzer
41   testing for the NCPD, and asked Avery to be ready at the station in case an Intoxilyzer needed
42   to be performed on Dawson. Then I walked back over to Hopson. At that point, Hopson really
43   started to open up to me about what happened that night. Since it was raining, I wasn't able to
44   take notes like I'd wanted at the scene, but I've included everything I remember Hopson tell-
45   ing me in either this affidavit or the FCT report of the crash that I created. Hopson was still

[Handwritten margin note near lines 3-6:] he said if he really thought he needed help, he would've stopped it

[Handwritten margin note near lines 35-37:] hadn't noticed slurred speech before

1   bleeding, and the EMTs finally talked Hopson into the ambulance. That was when I heard one
2   of the EMTs say that Vanessa had died.

3

4   It couldn't have been more than ten minutes since I'd arrived at the scene by that time, but it
5   seemed like a lifetime. At that point, it was just Dawson and I at the scene. Bennett had walked
6   back to Bennett's porch to give us some space. It was about that time that Vanessa Sullivan's
7   mother showed up on the scene. Ms. Sullivan was obviously devastated, but also really,
8   really angry. I told Ms. Sullivan that her daughter had been taken away, but Ms. Sullivan
9   insisted that she would be going nowhere yet. I believe her words were, "My daughter is *had*
10   dead because of this maniac! I never should have let Dawson anywhere near her. I can't *quote from*
11   bring Vanessa back, but I'm going to make Dawson's life a living hell because I can still do *DA, influ.*
12   that." Well, when the prosecutor talks like that, you know it's time to run a few tests. First, *cops actions*
13   I advised Dawson of Dawson's rights, and Dawson said, "I'm not drunk. You're just wasting
14   your time making me take those stupid tests. I can pass any test. Give me an LSAT question."
15   I told Dawson this was no time for jokes. Dawson was a little belligerent, but agreed to take
16   the field sobriety tests.

17

18   I started by having Dawson say the ABCs backwards starting with the letter "Q." While R and S
19   are letters, they are not before the letter Q, and they are certainly not before the letter M, which
20   is where Dawson put them. At that point, I decided it was time for a standard physical field
21   sobriety test. I was pretty sure what the result would be. Thankfully the rain had stopped, but
22   I still wanted to get away from the road. We went to Bennett's driveway, and I started the stan-
23   dard battery of field sobriety tests, which I have performed and interpreted hundreds of times,
24   so I'm pretty good at interpreting results. All observations and conclusions I'm writing about
25   are based on my extensive training and experience.

26   *DA was screaming @ Danny*
27   I asked Ms. Sullivan to stop screaming at Dawson and making Dawson nervous, but she ignored *The*
28   me. I then began the horizontal gaze nystagmus eye test. As is standard, I asked Dawson if *whole*
29   Dawson suffered from any neurological disorder that would cause nystagmus. Dawson said *time*
30   no and added, "I can see just fine. Can we get this over with?" I then moved forward with
31   the exam, taking my pen flashlight and shining it in the defendant's left eye and waiting for
32   sixty seconds to allow the pupil to adjust fully to the light.

33

34   Once Dawson's eye had adjusted, I moved my flashlight in the standard procedure and looked
35   for three signs of nystagmus: pronounced jerking in eye movement instead of a smooth move-
36   ment, inability to hold the eye in a set place without jerking when moved to and held at maxi-
37   mum deviation, and the angle at which jerking onsets when the eye is moving. I repeated this
38   process for the right eye. I noted all of the results and indicated that there were no environmen-
39   tal factors that would impact the test. Based on my training, the result of this test alone was
40   sufficient to conclude that the subject was intoxicated.

41   *his eyes made him look drunk*

42   Then I went on to the second test, in which Dawson had to walk heel-to-toe in a straight line
43   and follow my directions. Dawson stumbled several times and kept blaming it on the wet
44   pavement, but clearly failed that test. Dawson tripped every time I tried to get Dawson to turn
45   around and could barely walk in a straight line without falling. The ground was kind of slick.

on rainy road, when angry
woman screaming @ him

police officer
almost fell almost

1 I almost fell myself, but I'm still pretty sure Dawson was walking like Dawson was drunk, not
2 like Dawson was slipping. Finally, for the third test, I had Dawson stand on one leg and count
3 aloud starting at one thousand. Dawson complained again about the slick ground and kept using
4 both arms to balance. Dawson stopped counting several times and had to hop to keep from
5 falling. All of these were signs of intoxication.
6
7 Dawson had failed all three tests, so I was confident that Dawson was drunk. Of course,
8 Ms. Sullivan was yelling that she was going to need more evidence for a murder prosecution.
9 Officer Brady had arrived on the scene at that point, so I asked Brady to keep the scene secure
10 until I got back, and I drove Dawson to the station myself.
11
12 It took me about ten minutes to get to the station. When I arrived at the station with Dawson,
13 I helped Dawson into the station and onto a bench. I quickly briefed Captain Morrison on the
14 situation, but it seemed like Morrison had already been brought up to speed. Once they had

belligerent @ the station

15 checked Dawson in, Captain Morrison and I came out and helped Dawson back to a holding
16 cell. Dawson was a mess at this point, even worse than at the scene—trying to pull away from
17 us as we helped Dawson up, yelling angrily, and stumbling all over the place. Officer Ingman
18 (the junior officer on duty) and I managed to get Dawson back to the first holding cell after
19 some effort.
20
21 There was one other suspect in the cell with Dawson. I kept an eye on Dawson in the cell to
22 make sure Dawson didn't bother the other person in the cell (someone named Sandy Cullen,
23 who Morrison said was in for public intoxication). Dawson and Cullen sat and talked for a
24 few minutes, but Dawson's back was turned, and I couldn't hear what they were talking about.
25 Other than that, nothing notable happened until Smith and Ingman came and took Dawson,
26 presumably for the Intoxilyzer screen. I do not know what further tests, if any, were actually
27 administered, and I do not know the results. I did not want anyone else's tests to influence the
28 objectivity of my firsthand observations.
29
30 I returned to the scene immediately after that and went into the house to speak with Bennett.
31 Bennett seemed all out of sorts and kept talking about how we should have lowered the speed
32 limit to twenty-five on Canyon Road, but it was pretty clear from my talk with Bennett that
33 Dawson's drunk driving caused the accident. I could barely believe how intoxicated Dawson
34 was at the scene. I guess the rain must have made it hard to see how horribly Dawson was

big exclude?

35 driving when the car went past me.
36
37 I understand that Dawson is trying to blame the conditions and the design of Canyon Road for
38 the murder that Dawson committed when Dawson drove drunk that night. I have patrolled that
39 area for hundreds of nights, and under clear conditions, it is easy to navigate the Canyon Road
40 curve if you are going the speed limit or even a little faster. I have chased cars going sixty miles
41 an hour that have made the turn without even going onto the shoulder.
42
43 Sure, it was raining really hard that night. But that's no excuse not to drive safely. I was on
44 the taskforce that surveyed the safety of Canyon Road when Bennett started raising Cain
45 about the speed limit after those kids died when they drove off the road while intoxicated.

OR an animal spooked him

1   We watched drivers go around the curve in worse rain than the night when Vanessa Sullivan
2   died, and none of the drivers I observed had any problem navigating the curve. To go off the
3   road like Dawson, I think a driver would have to be really distracted, going really fast, or
4   really impaired.
5
6   My FCT report, which contains all of my conclusions about the accident reconstruction
7   I completed for this crash, confirms this. As you can see from my report, Dawson drove off
8   the right side of the road and made a rut of well over 100 feet. Then, Dawson swerved back
9   across to the road and hit a utility pole and tree that were a couple of feet off the other side
10 of the road. I calculated that Dawson was driving sixty-six miles per hour when Dawson
11 first lost control of the vehicle. That's more than thirty miles an hour faster than the posted
12 speed limit. Driving that speed would be unbelievably reckless given the darkness, heavy
13 rain, and reduced visibility due to weather conditions. I would say going that fast would
14 essentially be a suicide attempt if Dawson was also drunk. I understand that Leslie Roman,
15 who analyzed the crash for the defense, concluded that Dawson was only barely over the
16 speed limit. Roman generally does good work, but Roman's assumptions on this crash are
17 mistaken, as you can see from the differences between our reports. I agree with Roman
18 that the article by Windsor and Strasberg, "Vehicle Accident Reconstruction," is the only
19 treatise worth using in the field. I used the methods and drag sled described in the Windsor
20 and Strasberg primer. My calculations and conclusions regarding the vehicle's speed are
21 completely explained by the Windsor and Strasberg primer, and I relied on no other source
22 in making them.

validef. exp. is credible but her assump. wrong

23
24 I also understand from Roman's report that Dawson is claiming that a deer was in the car's
25 way. I interviewed three witnesses on the night of the crash, and none of them mentioned see-
26 ing a deer that night. This includes Dawson, who kept saying that Dawson had no idea why
27 the car behaved in the way it did and gave no explanation for what happened. To be fair, I did
28 once see a deer in that area about a year ago, but it's not like they are always on the road or
29 anything. Based on the statements I collected immediately after the accident and the lack of
30 any other evidence to confirm that a deer was there that night, I do not think there was a deer
31 on the road. I'm not surprised that Dawson claims to have seen one, though—anything to steer
32 blame away from where it belongs, which is on Dawson.
33
34 I provided a copy of the entire police file on this case to defense counsel prior to trial, and
35 I asked defense counsel if they had any more requests for discovery. They did not. The pros-
36 ecutors' office requires open-file discovery in Nita Center, and this case was no exception.
37
38 Of the affidavits and exhibits in this case, I am familiar with the following: Nita FCT Officer
39 Report, FCT Diagram, and Accident Photos 0001 through 0007, all of which I created; Bar Tab
40 #1 of Danny Dawson, Bar Tab #2 of Danny Dawson, and Bar Tab of Vanessa Sullivan, which
41 were collected from Chuggie's by Officer Baker and Officer Yarbough; the article "Vehicle
42 Accident Reconstruction: A Primer," which I relied upon in coming to my conclusions regard-
43 ing accident reconstruction; Curriculum Vitae of Leslie Roman, Expert Report of Leslie
44 Roman, Expert Report of Leslie Roman—Crime Scene Diagram, and Accident Photos 0008
45 through 0015, which were created by Leslie Roman and provided to me by counsel; the

1   Voicemail Message, which was obtained with the consent of the Sullivan family; my own
2   affidavit; and the affidavits of London Bennett, Leslie Roman, Taylor Hopson, Jordan James,
3   Pat Lawrence, and Sam Lyons, which I was provided by counsel.

I hereby attest to having read the above statement and swear or affirm it to be my own. I also swear or affirm to the truthfulness of its content. Before giving this statement, I was told it should contain everything I knew that might be relevant to my testimony, and I followed those instructions. I also understand that I can and must update this affidavit if anything new occurs to me until the moment before I testify in this case.

_____/s/ RKF_____
Ryan K. Foster

Subscribed and sworn before me on this, the 3rd day of October, YR-1.

_____/s/ SS_____
Sarah Shelton, Notary Public

AFFIDAVIT OF TAYLOR HOPSON

After being duly sworn upon oath, Taylor Hopson hereby deposes and states as follows:

1   My name is Taylor Hopson. I live in Nita Center, Nita, and I am a senior political science
2   major at Nita Center University. I was supposed to graduate in YR-1, but after what happened
3   last fall I had to take a leave of absence from school. I had always planned to stay in Nita and
4   go to law school, hopefully at Calkins Law with my best friend Vanessa, but now I just want
5   to get away from Nita and all the awful reminders of what happened. After this experience,
6   I don't want to be a lawyer anymore. I recently published a short story that helped get me
7   accepted into the prestigious Wasch School of Journalism at Herndon University in California,
8   and I can't wait to move away from Nita after this trial. I hope to write a story about this case
9   one day when I can come to terms with this terrible tragedy.
10
11   I first met the Sullivans when I was eight and my family moved into the house next door to
12   theirs. Ms. Sullivan was just a deputy prosecutor then, not famous like she is now. Vanessa and
13   I quickly discovered all the things we had in common, and in no time, we were inseparable.
14
15   Vanessa and I were both accepted to Calkins College in East Hill. I really wanted to go, but my
16   dad lost his job in YR-6, and I knew I would have to work through college just to pay for food
17   and books, no matter what kind of scholarships I got. I was happy that Vanessa got the chance
18   to go, though. I knew she was excited to get a little distance from Nita Center. Vanessa's parents
19   could be kind of strict, so they weren't really keen on her going far away to school. One time
20   during our junior year of high school, Vanessa got a little tipsy on some spiked punch at the
21   homecoming dance. It wasn't her fault at all, but she didn't want to drive home, so she had to
22   call her mom to come get her. When she showed up at the dance to get Vanessa, Ms. Sullivan
23   screamed at her in the parking lot for about fifteen minutes. She told Vanessa that she had no
24   right to embarrass her in public and asked how would it look if the DA's daughter had been
25   picked up on a public-intoxication charge. Vanessa just apologized and tried to explain that she
26   wasn't drunk, but it didn't matter to Ms. Sullivan. It was a long time before I ever saw Vanessa
27   drink alcohol again, and, whatever happened, she definitely didn't call her mom to pick her up.
28   Her dad came once when our designated driver got too trashed to drive home during fall break
29   of our freshman year of college. Usually, though, Vanessa just crashed at my house or made
30   sure we had a good designated driver.
31
32   To understand what happened on the night Vanessa died, I guess it helps to know why we were
33   even on Canyon Road at the time of the accident. Vanessa and I have a high-school friend who
34   has a pretty good career going as a musician. Our friend's band, Chatterbox, was playing a gig
35   at Chuggie's, right in our hometown the night of Vanessa's twenty-first birthday. Jordan James
36   tends the bar at Chuggie's and was going to be the opening act for the band. I knew James
37   from when I worked there, so it seemed like a great way to get two great shows in one night.
38   I called Vanessa to invite her to town for the show. She doesn't come home often, and the last
39   few times I tried to schedule a visit with her she was too busy. This time, though, she agreed
40   to come. I was so excited.

1   I was less excited when she called me back a few days later to make plans and told me her
2   college friend, Danny Dawson, was coming to town with her. I met Danny once before, but
3   Danny probably doesn't remember meeting me. I had visited Vanessa at Calkins College for a
4   weekend during our sophomore year. My last night in town, we went to a party at a local dive
5   bar in East Hill after a basketball game. Vanessa introduced Danny as someone in a lot of her
6   classes, and Danny sat and talked with us for a while. Danny seemed OK, but was already
7   pretty tipsy and kind of obnoxious. Later, when Vanessa and I were getting ready to drive back
8   to campus, we ran into Danny in the parking lot. By that point, Danny was full-on hammered
9   and barely walking straight. Some of Danny's friends tried to take Danny's keys away, but
10   Danny just shoved them off and shouted, "I'm not a baby. There are never cops on this road
11   after a home game. They know the fans like to celebrate. Stop being a buzzkill." Danny got
12   in the driver's seat of the car and drove away. The next day, Vanessa checked on Danny, and
13   I guess Danny made it home OK. I would never drive if I had even a single drink, but it seemed
14   then that maybe Danny knew how much Danny could handle better than I did. I didn't see
15   Danny again until Danny killed my best friend.
16

17   Vanessa came to pick me up around 6:45 p.m. We were supposed to drive together to Chuggie's
18   and meet Danny there. I didn't want to drive to the concert myself because I knew I would
19   probably want to have a drink or two to celebrate Vanessa's birthday. I don't usually drink
20   much, and I don't know my limits very well, so I never drive if I have anything to drink. I know
21   a lot of people drive after just a couple of drinks, and it isn't even illegal if you aren't drunk, but
22   I think that's just awful. I would never risk hurting someone else by being so selfish. Plus, my
23   car only seats two people, and I would never drive Vanessa's car because Ms. Sullivan would
24   kill me if she found out. She doesn't like anyone but Vanessa driving that car—something to do
25   with the insurance coverage. Besides, Vanessa said that since she drove Danny all the way to
26   town, Danny would be more than willing to be designated driver for the night. I asked Vanessa
27   if Danny planned to drink at all, and she said Danny swore not to have a sip. Just to be sure,
28   when we got to Chuggie's, I saw Danny and asked if Danny would play designated driver that
29   night while Vanessa and I got drunk. Danny said, "Lighten up, Taylor. Anybody can have a
30   drink or two and still be fine to drive. Besides, I'm here to see an awesome band, not to get
31   hammered. I doubt I'll have any more to drink. Don't worry about it." I was not exactly sure
32   what Danny meant by that, because Vanessa said Danny had sworn not to drink that night. But
33   I guess Danny had gotten to Chuggie's early and started celebrating without us. Still, I remem-
34   bered the previous incident from Calkins, and I believed Danny knew how to handle a night
35   out, so I decided to take Danny's word that everything would be OK. Trusting Danny was the
36   worst decision I have ever made.
37

38   Chuggie's is a neat little pub, about twenty minutes from my house. I actually worked there my
39   first two years of college to help pay for things my scholarship didn't cover. I had an internship
40   in D.C. the summer of YR-2, though, and I had not started back at my job when we went there
41   on September 24. Some of the wait staff was new, but the old regulars were still around, and
42   they still had the same taxi sitting out front. I was shocked to learn that Danny was also familiar
43   with Chuggie's. Apparently Danny had spent time in Nita Center during the summer I was in
44   D.C., and during that time, Danny practically lived at Chuggie's. Danny was more familiar with
45   some of the new staff, including the bartender, Jordan James, than I was. Jordan and I never

[handwritten margin note beside lines 10–16] instance of him driving drunk before

1 worked shifts together until right before I left for my internship. For the brief time we over-
2 lapped, I remember a lot of customers complained that Jordan made their drinks too weak, but
3 that Friday night was the first time I ever tasted a drink made by Jordan, and the drink seemed
4 very strong to me. *Very strong drinks → but she is biased*
5

6 Our table was in a perfect spot to see the stage. The lead singer of Chatterbox had actually
7 reserved it special for us, and there was a little card for Vanessa's birthday on the table. The
8 server, Pat Lawrence, was a really good waiter, too, constantly refilling our chip basket and
9 drinks before we could even ask for seconds. That was pretty amazing since Pat told us that
10 it was Pat's first day on the job. It was really great service, but I eventually had to tell Pat to
11 switch me to sweet tea. Since Pat was refreshing our drinks so fast, it was hard to tell how
12 many I had, but I was only a little lightheaded by the time I switched to tea, and I don't think
13 I had more than two or three full drinks with any alcohol in them. I started drinking tea about
14 twenty minutes before the band came on. *doesn't herself remember how many drinks she had*
15

16 Danny was a different story. As soon as we sat down, Danny ordered straight whiskey! Then
17 Danny tried to order shots for Vanessa and me, but I immediately declined. I never drink shots.
18 In fact, I never drink anything alcoholic other than screwdrivers (vodka and orange juice).
19 Vanessa agreed to do a shot with Danny, but only if it was a mild one. I think Pat brought a
20 lemon drop shot for Vanessa and Danny, and then Danny ordered a Nita Brown (a local beer
21 special to the pub), and I started getting really nervous about how much Danny was drinking
22 before we even got our cheese fries. I didn't want to keep bringing up the alcohol issue because
23 I didn't want to spend the whole night nagging Vanessa's friend, and I figured Danny had sev-
24 eral hours before the drive home, so I decided not to say anything. I was relieved that Danny
25 switched to sodas when the food came, and I tried to relax.
26

27 While we had dinner and waited for the band, I started to have a really good time. Danny was
28 much nicer than I originally expected and discussed the possibility of our all being at Calkins
29 Law the next year. Danny was even kind enough to spend a little time at the bar so Vanessa
30 and I could catch up and not feel silly talking about high-school friends. I don't remember
31 how long Danny was gone, but not long after Danny returned, Pat brought us a round of drinks
32 on the house in honor of Vanessa's birthday—whiskey-and-ginger-ale cocktails. They were
33 disgusting. I was annoyed because anybody at the bar other than Jordan would know me well
34 enough to never bring me whiskey, so I pushed mine aside. I don't know who ended up drink-
35 ing it, but it definitely wasn't me, and I know Vanessa isn't a fan of whiskey either. I assume
36 it was Danny. Danny was the only person at the table ordering whiskey by choice, and by the
37 time the band finished its first song, all the drinks on the table were empty. Then Danny started
38 ordering more drinks and told Pat to keep them coming strong. Danny kept buying me screw-
39 driver after screwdriver. I can't recall how many, but I know two things—I didn't drink them
40 all, and the glasses kept ending up empty in front of Danny.
41

42 When the band finished its first set, I went to the bathroom. The line was pretty long, so I
43 waited almost the whole length of the break, and by the time I got back I saw Danny was
44 strumming one of Chatterbox's guitars! I was appalled. Who picks up a guitar from a band on
45 break and starts pretending they're a rock star? Danny's playing was horrible, and Danny got

1   hustled off the stage by a bouncer. It was completely embarrassing. I thought Calkins students
2   were supposed to be smart, but Danny was acting really messed up by that point, and it was
3   all Vanessa could do to drag Danny back to the table. The band was cool about it, though, and
4   ordered our table another round of drinks. Then my friend suggested I join the band and sing
5   Vanessa's favorite song, Sunday Morning! I used to sing some in school, and I was really flat-
6   tered that the band wanted me to sing with them. Plus, I really wanted to get away from Danny,
7   so I left my complimentary screwdriver on the table and went to warm up a little before getting
8   on stage. Vanessa was really excited. Danny looked really annoyed.
9
10 While I was with the band I tried to keep an eye on the table so I could see just how many more
11 drinks Danny and Vanessa had, but the lights in the bar were pretty dim, and it was hard to make
12 out what was happening in the room. I could see the shapes of Vanessa and Danny at the table,
13 and Pat seemed to be making a lot of trips over, but I couldn't see what Pat was bringing. The
14 crowd loved our song so much that the band asked me to do another, so I sang two more songs
15 with them before heading back to the table.
16
17 By the time I got back, it was past midnight, and Vanessa was pretty buzzed. My screwdriver
18 was long gone, but I don't know if Danny drank it or if Pat just took it away. Danny looked
19 in bad shape, but when I tried to suggest we maybe take a cab home, Vanessa shouted, "No!
20 My mom will kill me if I leave my car here. You know how she gets when I've had even a tiny
21 bit of alcohol, and Danny's fine to drive. It'll be fine." I was really unhappy about trying to
22 drive home, and I should've fought harder to call someone or take the cab, but I could rarely say
23 no to Vanessa, so I just got in the car. Vanessa mentioned that we had to be back in ten minutes
24 or we would miss her curfew, and I was starting to freak out. I was especially worried because
25 I know that the drive from Chuggie's to Vanessa's is easily a twenty minute trip. I started
26 yelling at Danny that it was Danny's fault we had to stay so late, that Danny really should not
27 be driving, and that Vanessa was never going to get home in time. Danny laughed and said,
28 "Challenge accepted!" Danny said that Danny had made the drive in eight minutes before and
29 told me to get out my watch.
30
31 When we were walking (or in Danny's case, stumbling) to the parking lot, we walked past
32 the taxi stand. The taxi driver on duty, Sam Lyons, tried to get us to take the taxi home. Sam
33 even offered to bring Danny back the next day to pick up the car. But Danny just shoved Sam
34 away and said, "Nice try, but I'm not gonna give you two cab fares when I can manage a silly
35 ten-minute drive. Get lost." Danny should have listened. When we got to the car I was shaking
36 because I was scared, and I could tell Vanessa wasn't thrilled about letting Danny drive, but
37 neither of us felt good about driving the car either. Danny leaned over to me when unlocking
38 my door and tried to reassure me that everything was fine, but Danny's breath was awful and
39 reeked of liquor and stale beer. Then I saw Danny get in the car and pull out a radar detector.
40 I could not see where it came from, but I thought that Danny must be such a crazy driver that
41 Danny carries an illegal radar detector around in a back pocket or something. At that point,
42 I just wanted to get home without throwing up.
43
44 Danny was worried about taking the main roads back, in case we saw cops. Vanessa's mom
45 knows every cop in town, and getting pulled over would be a disaster for her, too, so I tried to

1   direct Danny on how to get to Vanessa's house on the back roads. By the time we got about
2   two miles off the main road, I knew we were in serious trouble. Danny was swerving all
3   over the place and going way too fast. I tried to tell Danny to slow down—the speed limit
4   was thirty-five miles per hour and it felt like we were going at least eighty—but Danny just
5   started yelling at me for being annoying and told me to stop being a nag. Canyon Road runs
6   all the way through town, but this part of it is actually off the beaten path. There are a lot of
7   trees around the curve, and the guardrails don't extend very far, so if you take the curves too
8   quickly, you can easily end up going off the road into the woods. Vanessa and I actually had
9   two people from our high school get killed there when we were growing up. Everyone in town
10   calls it the Death Zone. I tried again to tell Danny to slow down because the two-lane road
11   was getting curvier and the rain had picked up. When we got into the car at Chuggie's the rain
12   wasn't that bad, but now it was pouring. I told Danny that I was scared, and that turned out
13   to be a huge mistake. Danny responded that Danny was going to show me how Danny could
14   really drive. I said I wasn't trying to be a nag, and that I just didn't know if Danny could see
15   the lane change, but it didn't make a difference. Danny told me to go back to singing and said
16   that all my talking was distracting.

17

18   Danny also said it was hard to see and asked why our town didn't have any lights on the road.
19   It was true that the only light anywhere around came from London Bennett's house. It was so
20   hard to see, but there was nothing in front of the car but rain. I have seen a deer on the side of
21   Canyon road maybe once or twice when I was in high school, but there definitely wasn't a deer
22   or anything like what Danny is claiming happened that night.

23

24   By this point, Vanessa was clutching the armrests of the front seat and looked pretty green.
25   I started to worry that she was going to vomit all over the dashboard. I tried again to tell Danny
26   to slow down because the road was going to get narrower, but Danny refused. I think Danny
27   was swerving just to spite me. Vanessa tried to get Danny to slow down by telling Danny she
28   would just call her dad to tell him we would be little late. I remember her saying, "You don't
29   have to risk getting pulled over just to get me home by 1:00. I'll just call my dad, Danny. Slow
30   down." Danny didn't seem to hear her and just turned the music up louder.

31

32   That's when Vanessa called her dad. The music was so loud it was hard to hear everything
33   she said, but right in the middle of the call I remember Danny swerving the car across the
34   road for what seemed like no reason. I was terrified, and so was Vanessa, and she told Danny
35   to knock it off. But Danny started weaving again and this time it was a huge miscalculation
36   because when Danny tried to go back on the road, the car just started sliding. I remember
37   screaming as we spun in a circle, and my stomach dropped, but I couldn't tell where we
38   were going. Then everything went black. I have heard the recording that Vanessa left for her
39   dad that night. I can't imagine how he felt when he heard it because it is obvious from that
40   message that Danny is to blame and that's the last thing her parents, or any of us, will ever
41   hear her say.

42

43   It is hard to remember things after the crash very clearly. I don't think I passed out, but I don't
44   really remember anything from that point on very well. I don't even know how I got out of
45   the car, but I do remember lots of blood everywhere. Everything was red, and I was soaked

1   from the rain. There were flashing blue lights all around us and the sound of horns. Someone
2   was talking to me and telling me not to move. The next thing I remember was waking up in a
3   hospital room. My mom and dad were there. I asked them if Vanessa was OK, and my mom just
4   started crying and shaking her head. I didn't ask about Danny because I didn't care if Danny
5   was dead. I know that sounds horrible, but this was Danny's fault.
6

7   The next time I saw Danny was on September 29 at Vanessa's funeral. There were a million
8   people there; everybody loved Vanessa. It was a beautiful service. But when we got to the
9   cemetery, there was Danny Dawson, standing alongside a tree overlooking the gravesite. I was
10   furious, but I didn't want to make a scene with Vanessa's family there. I walked up to Danny
11   and said, "I can't believe you would have the nerve to show up to Vanessa's funeral after you
12   murdered her. You need to leave." Danny looked me in the eye and said, "Look, she was my
13   friend, too. Besides, it's not my fault a deer ran into the road." I was shocked. I couldn't believe
14   what I had just heard. I said to Danny, "What are you talking about? There was no deer in the
15   road!" Danny just glared at me and said, "Prove it." I wanted to hit Danny at that point, but for-
16   tunately, Danny also chose that moment to leave the funeral and the family in peace. If anyone
17   should have been buried in that cemetery, it was Danny, not Vanessa. Instead, I ended up in a
18   hospital for two days and Vanessa is dead. I didn't suffer any lasting physical injuries from the
19   crash, but the scar of losing Vanessa will never heal. Danny walked away without a scratch.
20   I hope Danny goes away to jail forever. What kind of life should someone have after murdering
21   an innocent girl?
22

23   Of the available exhibits in this case, I am familiar with the following: Bar Tab #1 of Danny
24   Dawson, Bar Tab #2 of Danny Dawson, and Bar Tab #3 of Vanessa Sullivan, which were
25   signed by the indicated parties in my presence on September 24 and 25, YR-2; Accident Pho-
26   tos 0001 through 0015, which were shown to me by attorneys and which I agree are accurate
27   depictions of the images contained therein; and the Voicemail Message, which was provided
28   to me by attorneys. I can confirm that the speaking voice on the Voicemail Message belongs to
29   Vanessa Sullivan, and that the Voicemail Message is the recording of the call made by Vanessa
30   that I reference in this affidavit. I am also familiar with the Chuggie's Drink Menu, and except
31   where specifically noted elsewhere in my affidavit, I have no reason to believe that any of the
32   drinks served at Chuggie's on September 24 or 25, YR-2, either omitted a component listed or
33   added a component not listed on the drink menu. I am not familiar with any other exhibits or
34   any affidavits other than my own.

I hereby attest to having read the above statement and swear or affirm it to be my own and
consistent with the testimony provided during my grand jury testimony. I also swear or affirm
to the truthfulness of its content. Before giving this statement, I was told to include everything
I knew that might be relevant to the events described related to these charges. I also understand
that I can and must update this affidavit if anything new occurs to me until the date of my trial
in this case. I have also read and am familiar with the statements I provided to police officers

and law enforcement officers related to these events and confirm that all documents showing my signature reflect my genuine signature.

_____/s/ TJH_____
Taylor J. Hopson

Subscribed and sworn before on this, the 3rd day of October, YR-2.

_____/s/ SS_____
Sarah Shelton, Notary Public

Affidavit of Jordan James

After being duly sworn upon oath, Jordan James hereby deposes and states as follows.

1   My name is Jordan James. I grew up in Chicago, Illinois, and went to Marquette University
2   on a music scholarship after high school. I left Marquette after three years and never earned
3   a degree. It always seemed to me that there were better moneymaking opportunities out there
4   for me than staying in college. For example, I found out that I was one heck of a bartender,
5   and with my musical talents, the money made tending bar and performing on the side was
6   incredibly good—better than almost any other job I could get. I took my talents down south
7   to the beach and worked at a famous tourist trap. I was making phenomenal money, but I was
8   spending it faster than I could make it, so I decided to move to somewhere with a lower cost
9   of living a little while back. That somewhere was Nita Center.
10
11   Since moving back in the spring of YR-2, I have been tending bar and playing occasional
12   gigs at Chuggie's. It's a great place to work and to hang out, if that's your thing. It's great
13   for me because I can use my musical ability to make some extra bucks on top of bartending,
14   and the owner lets me keep my hair any way I want as long as the customers keep coming
15   back. Chuggie's has a little something for everyone. We have live music four nights a week
16   (I usually do a few songs and pick up a bunch of tips before the main act), karaoke every other
17   night, and even a 3-D TV to replace that old human darts game. The main attraction, of course,
18   is all the liquor you can afford. From beer to the hard stuff, we've got it, and we want you to
19   buy it! That is how I make most of my money, of course; people come in to have a good time,
20   and I make that happen by serving up strong drinks and music requests. If they have a good
21   time and like my service, they will give me a tip. In my experience, the drunker they are, the
22   better my songs sound and the bigger my tip gets. Every bartender knows the gulp-to-green
23   correlation, and we do our best to make sure our bills get paid. I would never spike a drink or
24   anything like that, of course, but it's nice that the bar doesn't make us measure our pours.
25
26   I met Danny Dawson at the bar during the summer of YR-2. Danny came in one night with a
27   bunch of friends. I was between sets and serving some drinks. Danny came right over to me and
28   ordered a Blackout, our most intoxicating drink. I knew right away Danny was a "rainmaker."
29   You see, every bartender has a pool of great customers to rely on for steady income. We keep
30   them happy, and they keep us happy. Regular customers like Danny can account for as much
31   as half of my tips in a month, and Danny did not disappoint. Over the summer when Danny
32   was in town, I would say Danny tipped me nearly $750, though the IRS has certainly taken its
33   share. Danny was probably my biggest tipper. I returned the favor by making Danny's drinks
34   just the way Danny likes them, with more liquor than the average drink. Danny says there's no
35   point in messing around with all the extra juice and calories in lots of mixed drinks. Besides,
36   Danny would rather drink one drink that has the liquor of two than be hassled with having to
37   drink two drinks. In my experience, Danny's drinking habits usually coincide with that.
38
39   Aside from being a great customer, Danny has always been a very nice person to me and
40   most of the patrons at the bar. Danny has never been involved in a fight or even so much as

1 a shouting match with another customer. Danny also possesses one character trait that makes
2 Danny pretty much unique at our bar—Danny is conscientious about not driving drunk. I'll
3 put it this way: Danny may have a drinking problem, but Danny does not have a drinking and
4 driving problem. I can't even count or remember all the times over the past two years that
5 Danny has voluntarily handed over the keys to Danny's car to a friend or taken a taxi cab home.
6 When I close, I am typically leaving the bar at 8:00 a.m., but the patrons go home much earlier.
7 There have been dozens of occasions where Danny has left the bar in a taxi cab, and I run into
8 Danny at 8:00 a.m. while I am leaving and see Danny, then completely sobered up, pulling back
9 up in a taxi cab to retrieve Danny's car that Danny left the night before because Danny was too
10 drunk. I wish all our customers took that same approach.
11
12 I also was in a summer softball league with Danny. I signed up for a local team, and lo and
13 behold, on the first day of practice Danny was there on the same team. We became good bud-
14 dies over the course of that summer, what with all the practices, games, and pizza-and-beer
15 celebrations after our victories. I hate to say this about Danny, but to be quite honest, sober or
16 not, Danny is not the most coordinated person. We always joked about it on the team by asking
17 where the other two stooges were. Danny struggled to swing a softball bat without falling down
18 face first into the dirt. Sometimes Bosh, the captain of the team, would joke that Danny was the
19 most likely person on the team to get a wrongful DUI conviction just because Bosh couldn't
20 imagine Danny ever being able to pass a field sobriety test. We had a local cop named Dirk on
21 our team who carried Bosh's joke a bit too far one day after a game and tested Danny. He never
22 told us if Danny passed or failed the test, but it didn't look to me like Danny did too well for
23 being stone-cold sober.
24
25 The night that poor girl died, I was working at the bar, both serving and being the opening
26 musical act. In fact, I started serving at around noon. Danny came in pretty early that day and
27 said something about a job interview. I tried my best to listen, but I was pretty busy that after-
28 noon training Pat Lawrence for the evening shift. Pat did not stick around the job very long,
29 and I do not remember anything about Pat other than the fact that I trained Pat that afternoon.
30 Danny was drinking some that afternoon, but Danny told me that Danny was not driving
31 anywhere that night, so I was not too worried. Apparently Danny had already arranged for a
32 ride home.
33
34 I can't say I remember the details from later that night as clearly as I wish I could. I was run-
35 ning around like a chicken with my head cut off keeping up with all of the orders. I pulled in
36 several hundred dollars in tips that night, which is on par with New Year's Eve for me. I think
37 Danny drank much less than usual that night. I barely remember sending any drinks over to
38 Danny's table that evening, and I don't remember anyone else getting them drinks. I know that
39 Danny came up to the bar with a friend, and I gave those two a shot and a beer because that's
40 what I do for loyal customers to keep tips high. I also think someone sent a round of drinks to
41 Danny's table because it was the birthday of the girl who passed away. The only other drink
42 I remember was when I did a shot with Danny myself. I would estimate that Danny had about
43 two or three more drinks. Of course, Danny bought probably at least twice that much alcohol,
44 but the other half was sent to various patrons as per Danny's typical routine. Danny was always
45 flirting or schmoozing!

1   I remember Danny coming to the bar and asking for some darts. I knew this was trouble, but
2   not because Danny was drunk—in fact, Danny's speech wasn't slurred at all. I was worried
3   because Chuggie's was so crowded. You see, Danny cannot even throw darts straight when
4   Danny is sober, so it's a bad idea for Danny to be tossing around sharp objects in a crowd.
5   I diplomatically took the darts away, and it was no big deal. When I took the dart, Danny
6   laughed, "Are you sure that dart board's not moving? I guess I'm just way off tonight, Jordan."
7   Maybe Danny was already buzzed at that point, but I could not really be sure. I remember
8   Danny getting up and strumming the guitar, and Danny was pretty good as usual. The whole
9   crowd cheered as Danny left the stage. *Danny was perceived favorably by crowd*
10

11   From what I remember, Danny was there with two friends. One was the birthday girl, who
12   unfortunately passed away, and the other was Taylor Hopson, who worked at Chuggie's back
13   when I started. I never really knew Taylor that well, except I was warned that Taylor would
14   basically take keys away from anyone who had a beer. That's not really a good fit for someone
15   working at a bar—talk about a buzzkill! That came back to me pretty quickly when I heard
16   Taylor and Danny arguing about who was going to drive. I think Danny was claiming that *special.*
17   Taylor was supposed to drive, and Taylor said that was the plan before, but now Taylor was
18   just too drunk and said they should take a cab instead. I heard Danny respond that Danny was
19   OK and pronounce that they would be home in record time.
20

21   That happened right before the three of them left. I don't really remember what time Danny
22   left, but I do remember Danny coming to settle up. It was well after midnight, and the bar had
23   started to die down a bit. Danny came up and asked me what the damage was. I handed Danny
24   the receipt, and Danny signed it and left me a big tip, a little bit more than normal even for
25   Danny. I do vaguely remember another patron asking if Danny wanted a shot for the road, but
26   I can't say whether or not Danny took him up on the offer.
27

28   The police later came and asked for the bar's copy of Danny's and Vanessa Sullivan's tabs
29   from that night, and I handed them over to them. I have since been shown the exhibits, and
30   they are in the same condition they were when I handed them over to the police. The tab does
31   not include any complimentary drinks because those are not recorded. By the time the police
32   came back and asked for everyone else's bar tab from that night, the records had been deleted.
33   Nobody told us to hold onto them. I do remember that once Danny signed the bill, Danny
34   winked at me and said, "Thanks again for pouring them strong and long." Danny then walked
35   away with the two friends, and, well, the rest we all know.
36

37   I never found out who drove that night or anything like that. I can't imagine Danny would have
38   driven if Danny were too drunk—that would just be so out of character for Danny. Danny's
39   always been a good customer, and hopefully once this all blows over, I'll see Danny back at
40   Chuggie's sometime soon.
41

42   Of the affidavits and exhibits in this case, I am familiar with the following: Bar Tab #1 of
43   Danny Dawson, Bar Tab #2 of Danny Dawson, and Bar Tab #3 of Vanessa Sullivan, which
44   were provided by me to the Nita Police Department and which I can identify as standard
45   Chuggie's receipts. I am also familiar with the Chuggie's Drink Menu, and except where

1   specifically noted elsewhere in my affidavit, I have no reason to believe that any of the drinks
2   served at Chuggie's on September 24 or 25, YR-2, either omitted a component listed or added a
3   component not listed on the drink menu. I am not familiar with any other exhibits or affidavits
4   other than my own.

I hereby attest to having read the above statement and swear or affirm it to be my own. I also swear or affirm to the truthfulness of its content. Before giving this statement, I was told it should contain everything I knew that might be relevant to my testimony, and I followed those instructions. I also understand that I can and must update this affidavit if anything new occurs to me until the moment before I testify in this case.

_____/s/ JJ_____
Jordan James

Subscribed and sworn before me on this, the 3rd day of October, YR-2.

_____/s/ LJK_____
L. James King, Notary Public

AFFIDAVIT OF PAT LAWRENCE

After being duly sworn upon oath, Pat Lawrence hereby deposes and states as follows.

1 My name is Pat Lawrence. I lost my job in the first part of the recession, and I would rather not
2 talk about my employment history. I always figured a college degree would be good enough to
3 get me a solid job, but I found out that hardly anybody was hiring when I graduated. My job
4 got outsourced, and I found myself looking for a job. I thought about running for Congress, but
5 I decided that was beneath me. Instead, I decided to apply for a job as a server at Chuggie's.
6 I was hired on Wednesday, September 22, YR-2. My first shift was that Friday night. I showed
7 up at work that afternoon to do a little training. That's when I first met Danny Dawson.
8
9 Dawson told me something about being in town for a job interview, but I figured that Dawson
10 was interviewing to be an alcoholic. Who puts back half a dozen alcoholic drinks in the middle
11 of the day? I did not actually serve any of them, but I saw that our bartender, Jordan James, just
12 kept putting more liquor in front of Dawson, and the glasses kept emptying. It is possible that
13 James was drinking some of them, but James explained to me that James never drinks on the
14 job, especially not early in the day.
15
16 I actually had a long chat with James, who let me know that I really needed to keep an eye out
17 for drunk people pushing their limits that Friday night. Apparently, the owner of Chuggie's was
18 trying to draw in some new business since Chatterbox was going to be playing at Chuggie's
19 that night and asked James to pour the drinks much, much stronger than usual. It sounded to
20 me like the drinks were usually pretty weak. On the day of my interview, I even think I heard
21 the owner say, "We're going to serve more water and less alcohol in our drinks because we're
22 going to make more profit. Water down those liquor bottles before the customers arrive so no
23 one suspects anything!" ⟶ drinks strong
24
25 I did not actually start waiting tables until around 7:00 p.m. that night. It's a good thing it
26 was not any sooner. Around 6:30, Dawson stumbled toward a table from the bar and dropped
27 Dawson's drink. It spilled all over me. Luckily I had gone to buy clothes for work that morn-
28 ing and was able to run to my car to grab a change of clothes. I can't say I was too excited to
29 learn after I changed that Dawson was going to be in my section. Dawson was joined by two
30 other friends. I do not really remember much about either of them. I now know that the one
31 celebrating her birthday was Vanessa Sullivan, and I am told that the other friend's name is
32 Taylor Hopson. As soon as I got to the table, Dawson was ready to order more alcohol. I did
33 not know how much longer Dawson was going to make it. Dawson ordered a whiskey on the
34 rocks for Dawson and a round of shots for the others. Dawson also ordered appetizers for
35 the table, including a massive order of cheese fries. Dawson asked me to get James to make
36 the drink on the strong side, which I already knew was going to happen.
37
38 I was relieved when the entire table switched to drinking soda and sweet tea for a while.
39 Hopson was pretty excited that we had sweet tea and started complaining about how they

1   should have it everywhere. I told the table that the designated driver was going to get free sodas
2   and asked who that was going to be. It was so quiet at the table that you could hear a pin drop.
3   Dawson's hand went up, and I laughed pretty hard. Hopson and Vanessa Sullivan must not have
4   thought it was a very funny joke. I figured one of them had to be the DD.
5
6   I lost track of Dawson for a while as Hopson and Vanessa Sullivan kept chatting away at the
7   table. They were starting to act pretty drunk, and I was starting to worry about the table a bit.
8   I caught Dawson drinking a shot at the bar out of the corner of my eye I think, but I am not
9   sure about that. When I went back over toward the bar to pick up some drinks, James handed
10   me three whiskey-and-ginger-ale drinks "on the house" to send over to Dawson's table. I took
11   them over there, and only Dawson really seemed excited about them. I saw Dawson drink all
12   of one of the whiskey drinks, and I think I saw Dawson sipping on both of the others. I know
13   the drinks were empty when I got over there later, and I never saw Hopson or Vanessa Sullivan
14   take a sip.
15
16   Chatterbox started playing, and Vanessa Sullivan and Dawson were the only two people left
17   at the table; Hopson was on stage singing. Dawson insisted that I bring Dawson and Vanessa
18   some mixed drinks to celebrate Vanessa's birthday. I must have brought over three screwdrivers
19   for each of them while Hopson was on stage. I think Dawson may have consumed a little more
20   than Dawson's share of them because Vanessa looked like she was struggling by the second
21   one. I was pretty sure that Hopson was going to be the designated driver though, so it was going
22   to be OK.
23
24   A little while later, I noticed Dawson standing alone over in the corner of the dining area.
25   I asked Dawson if Dawson wanted anything else, and Dawson asked for a tequila sunrise
26   because Dawson wanted the night to never end. I could tell Dawson was pretty drunk, so I said
27   "OK, as long as you're not driving home." Dawson shot back that Dawson was not even that
28   tipsy. Dawson said to bring a tequila sunrise and then bring sodas for the rest of the night.
29   Dawson then started railing about how Dawson had never been so buzzed before with so few
30   drinks and that Dawson had to be imagining it. I told Dawson that James was pouring incred-
31   ibly strong drinks. Dawson laughed and said that Chuggie's has the wateriest drinks in town,
32   but at least Dawson got a good deal with all of the drinks that never made it on to the bar tab.
33   Dawson informed me that Dawson always got "strong" drinks from James, which meant a
34   normal drink at any other bar. I tried to convince Dawson that Dawson was wrong, but Dawson
35   was having none of it. I brought the tequila sunrise and started running sodas over as quickly
36   as possible. Dawson really did not need to get behind the wheel.
37
38   Dawson pulled me over to the side when I brought the last soda over to Dawson. Dawson
39   asked me if I "had any pills, you know, to help me focus on the drive home." I had no clue
40   what Dawson was talking about, but Dawson claimed to have heard that the servers at
41   Chuggie's usually had those ADD pills or something to help people focus and that Dawson
42   was really going to need help focusing on the ride home. I had no idea what Dawson was
43   talking about, and I did not tell anybody about that conversation, especially not the police.
44   I was worried that they might investigate me or something, even though I did not do any-
45   thing wrong.

[handwritten margin note, left side:] usually pour weak drinks, how it vearrangle for him to think they were weak or strong?

1   The lead singer for Chatterbox and Dawson's friends joined us about that time, and Dawson
2   went silent. Somebody from the band ordered shots for everyone. Dawson whispered to me
3   that Dawson just wanted shots of water. I think I really, really messed that one up. I did pour
4   one shot of water, but I forgot which one it was by the time I got back. You see, the shots were
5   grain alcohol shots, which look just like water, but are twice as alcoholic as normal shots
6   of liquor. Judging by everyone's reaction, I think that Hopson got the water shot. I say that
7   because I know grain alcohol burns, and everyone else reacted pretty visibly. Realizing my
8   mistake, I told Dawson what happened immediately and begged Dawson not to drive. Dawson
9   said that Dawson was just fine, that the grain alcohol would help Dawson's driving, and that
10 Dawson would call the bar after setting a speed record on the way back to Vanessa Sullivan's
11 home. I wouldn't say that Dawson was sober before the grain-alcohol shot. In fact, I'd say
12 Dawson was pretty drunk. But I could tell that Dawson still was kind of with it, and I could see
13 how Dawson would think that Dawson was OK. Dawson was not acting a total fool anymore,
14 but Dawson was slurring and stumbling a good bit before I made a huge mistake of effectively
15 giving Dawson two shots on the way out the door.
16   *huge mistake of giving him extra shots*

17 Realizing my mistake could be pretty serious when I saw pictures of the heavy rain on a TV
18 in the bar, I knew I needed to do something. It was too late by the time I got outside. I heard
19 Dawson yell at someone that Dawson would make Richard Petty seem like he belonged in the
20 slow lane by the time they got to Vanessa's house. My heart sank. As you know, Richard Petty
21 is a famous race-car driver. I expected that Hopson and Vanessa Sullivan would refuse to get
22 in the car. Instead, Hopson just said that Hopson was pretty sure that Hopson could make the   *Pursues*
23 drive even faster and asked for the keys. I thought maybe Hopson was trying to trick Dawson   *super*
24 into handing over the keys, but before I knew it I heard Dawson say, "No way," and the car   *drunk*
25 was off. I guess I kind of froze while everyone was screaming. I really should have got to the
26 car and stopped that terrible tragedy from happening. Even if the drinks served to Dawson
27 were weak, there's no way Dawson should have been driving a car that night. As strong as they
28 were, I am fairly surprised Dawson did not pass out before Dawson ever got in the car.
29
30 That Friday night was my first and last as an employee of Chuggie's. Vanessa Sullivan's mother   *biased in*
31 came in and said that she was going to take the bar's liquor license for killing her daughter. The *his*
32 owner told Ms. Sullivan that I had confessed to messing everything up and serving way too   *account*
33 much to Dawson. Then, the owner told Ms. Sullivan that I had been fired. Ms. Sullivan said   *b/c he*
34 she would make sure I never worked in Nita Center again. I had actually never said a word   *was*
35 to the owner. I can't believe I got thrown under the bus like that. I hope that Chuggie's goes   *blamed +*
36 out of business, and I have written Ms. Sullivan to tell her that I want to help her shut down   *fired*
37 Chuggie's. She has yet to return my calls, but I expect that once the people of Nita Center hear
38 about the strong drinks that night and the possibility that the staff was dealing drugs, I will be
39 needed for a pretty important investigation.
40
41 Of the exhibits in this case, I am familiar with the following: Bar Tab #1 of Danny Dawson,
42 which I can identify as a standard Chuggie's receipt; and Bar Tab #2 of Danny Dawson and
43 Bar Tab of Vanessa Sullivan, which I can identify as standard Chuggie's receipts for orders
44 placed through me on September 24 and 25, YR-2. I am also familiar with the Chuggie's Drink
45 Menu, and except where specifically noted in my affidavit, I have no reason to believe that any

1   of the drinks served on the night of September 24 either omitted a component listed or added a
2   component not listed on the drink menu. I am not familiar with any other exhibits or affidavits
3   other than my own.

I hereby attest to having read the above statement and swear or affirm it to be my own. I also swear or affirm to the truthfulness of its content. Before giving this statement, I was told it should contain everything I knew that might be relevant to my testimony, and I followed those instructions. I also understand that I can and must update this affidavit if anything new occurs to me until the moment before I testify in this case.

_____/s/ PAL_____
Pat A. Lawrence

Subscribed and sworn before me on this, the 3rd day of October, YR-2.

_____/s/ SS_____
Sarah Shelton, Notary Public

Affidavit of Sam Lyons

After being duly sworn upon oath, Sam Lyons hereby deposes and states as follows.

1   My name is Sam Lyons. I am currently a cab driver for the AAA Cab Company—"the first
2   name in personal transportation services"—right here in Nita Center. I have been driving cabs
3   for the last four years while trying to go back and get my college degree. Of course, as one
4   of the newer cabbies, I've been working the third shift, so I've probably slept through more
5   classes than I've attended—not counting the classes I've attended and slept through, that is.
6

7   My usual pickup spot during the night is at Chuggie's. I worked there waiting tables one sum-
8   mer, so I know the owner, and I'm the cabbie of choice for the more responsible falling-down
9   drunks that frequent the establishment. I have my share of regulars that depend on me to get
10   them home after a few too many. They make a mess of the back of my cab occasionally, but
11   they always tip really well when that happens.
12

13   On September 24, YR-2, I showed up to Chuggie's at about 4:30 p.m. to grab a burger and
14   a couple of cups of coffee while it was still too early for anyone to be too drunk to drive.
15   Chuggie's does a good lunch business during the day, and their coffee is surprisingly good—
16   and they have a liquor license, so you can get your coffee Irish anytime after noon!
17

18   It was a Friday afternoon, so it was pretty empty except for a few stragglers from the after-
19   noon lunch crowd and a few others there to get a jump on the night ahead. Jordan James, the
20   bartender, was working the bar and training a new server named Pat Lawrence. Danny Dawson
21   was there when I arrived, and I said hello. Danny is one of my frequent flyers in the cab, espe-
22   cially during the summer. Danny tends to be very talkative after having a few too many, and as
23   a result, let's just say Danny had a lot of occasions to be very talkative in my cab over the few
24   months prior to that night. I wouldn't say we're friends, but Danny has always tipped me well.
25

26   Danny is a student at Calkins College, and Danny had just come back from an interview for
27   a summer internship—some friend of a friend had a connection, but apparently the interview
28   didn't go well, according to Danny. While I was there, Danny ordered a drink—I think it was
29   a rum and soda. Jordan came over and set it down right next to two more empty glasses just
30   like it. Danny offered to buy me a drink, and called Jordan over. Jordan gave me a heads-up
31   that tonight would be a busy night for me—Nita's own Chatterbox was playing a tune-up show
32   before a nationwide tour, and the place was going to be packed to the rafters. I joked with
33   Jordan that I'd better start drinking then, and Jordan grabbed me a big to-go paper cup and
34   poured me my brew of choice—a large Colombian coffee, straight, no chaser.
35

36   I stayed and chatted with Danny for a few more minutes. Danny definitely seemed buzzed,
37   so when I left I told Danny, "You know where to find me, right?" so that Danny knew I'd be
38   outside to offer a ride home later. Danny said, "Nah, DD's gonna be the DD tonight! Ha, get
39   it?" I thought Danny was joking that Danny was planning to be the designated driver, since

he admitted HE was supposed to be DD

1   Danny's speech was already slurred. I laughed and headed out the door, grabbing my coffee and
2   heading out to get a newspaper to pass the time.
3
4   I got back to Chuggie's around 7:00 p.m. and hung out at the bar for a while, watching the
5   crowd start to gather. Jordan, the bartender, was playing an opening set for the band. Appar-
6   ently Chatterbox has quite a following in Nita, because the place got pretty packed by the time
7   they started their first set. The music wasn't really anything exciting to me, but there were obvi-
8   ously some diehard fans there, including Danny.
9
10   By getting there early, Danny had scored a table just off to the side of the dance floor, first table
11   from the stage. Danny had a couple of friends along for the show and was clearly enjoying
12   the evening. One of the friends was a woman I didn't recognize, but that I later found out was
13   Vanessa Sullivan, the prosecutor's daughter who died in the wreck. I recognized the other one
14   right away as Taylor Hopson. I liked to think of Taylor as a cabbie's perfect wingman because
15   Taylor was paranoid about people driving after having a couple of beers. Taylor is always tell-
16   ing people to take a cab home, which is great for my business. Taylor can be a pain though. One
17   time Taylor saw me drinking a beer early in the evening, well before any of the patrons would
18   be looking for a ride home. Taylor went right to the bartender and said I shouldn't be served any
19   more alcohol and I shouldn't be allowed to drive a cab that night! The joke was on Taylor—
20   I was drinking a non-alcoholic brew that time. I don't get behind the wheel if I feel even a little
21   bit buzzed—it's not worth the risk.
22
23   While the bands played, Pat was plenty busy bringing rounds of drinks and food to Danny's
24   table, and Danny was dancing like a demented marionette from the moment Chatterbox hit the
25   stage. About five songs into Chatterbox's set, I knew it was about time to be getting back to the
26   cab to get ready for the first of the evening's fares. I settled into my cab to read the paper and
27   wait for business to pick up.
28
29   At about 11:00 p.m., I came back inside Chuggie's to use the restroom and then returned to the
30   counter to get another cup of coffee for the road. When I got to the bar, Danny was standing
31   there, obviously having ordered something and looking anxious to get back to the band. Danny
32   grabbed me by the arm excitedly and yelled in my ear, "Thisssh hash to be the best night of
33   my life! Wooooo!" I thought that was weird—Danny was down about the interview before, but
34   I guess between the band and the booze it had turned around. I smiled and said, "I guess I'll be
35   seeing you out front in a bit, right?" Danny just laughed loudly and didn't answer, but from the
36   look in Danny's eyes and how slurred Danny's speech was, I figured there was no way Danny
37   was driving home that night. Danny didn't make a habit of driving drunk—that's why Danny
38   was one of my best customers. I remembered Danny's "DD" comment from when we talked
39   earlier that afternoon, but figured maybe Danny was just making a play on words. I figured
40   whatever the plan was, Danny was drunk now and would be in the back of the cab before the
41   evening was through. I watched the bartender pour out three "Chuggie Bombs"—the infamous
42   energy-drink-and-liqueur—and what I'm pretty sure was a rum and soda, though it was hard to
43   see exactly what went into the glass because someone pushed into me at the bar. Danny gulped
44   down one of the Chuggie Bombs, gathered up the three remaining glasses from the order, and
45   headed back to the table by the stage.

1   I went out to the cab at about 11:20 p.m. and waited a few minutes before I got my first fare
2   of the night. After a few round-trips shuttling home well-saturated patrons, I arrived back in
3   front of Chuggie's at about 12:40 a.m. to wait for another fare. There had been a thunderstorm
4   threatening for the last hour or so, and it was starting to roll in. There was some rain after
5   midnight—I was using my wipers on the way back to Chuggie's, but the heavy stuff didn't
6   come down until about fifteen minutes or so after I had gotten back. Danny came out of the
7   bar with the two other people that had been at Danny's table when I saw them earlier. I called
8   out to Danny and said, "You ready to go?" Now, my cab's a hybrid—Nita gave a bunch of tax
9   incentives as part of an environmental initiative, or maybe some state rep's brother owned a
10   car dealership and needed some sales—so it's not big, but there's enough room for three to
11   squeeze in the back or two in the back and one in the front. I started shifting stuff out of the
12   front seat to make room, but Danny looked in for a moment and appeared to be thinking, then
13   said, "No, we're good. Besides, you drive too slow!" Danny laughed and walked away with
14   the two friends. Danny sounded better than earlier at the bar—I don't think Danny could have
15   put those sentences together a couple of hours before. Still, I figured that girl Vanessa must
16   be driving. But I saw Danny open the doors of a Chevy Impala for the two passengers before
17   getting in the driver's seat. The car sped off quickly and screeched and fishtailed on the wet
18   pavement as it exited the parking lot with Danny behind the wheel.
19

20   I read about the accident in the paper the next day. The weather was pretty bad that night, and
21   from what the paper said about where the crash happened on Canyon Road, they were on a
22   pretty bad stretch of road in a wooded area. The part of Canyon Road where they crashed has a
23   banked curve, and there's a yellow deer-crossing sign a little while before it. The posted speed
24   limit there is thirty-five, though I have to admit I've driven it faster on a few occasions. It's a
25   fun stretch of road when it's light outside, it's dry, and you know what you're doing and where
26   the speed traps are. But it is also a dangerous road and has definitely been the spot of more
27   than a few accidents. I remember talking to Danny about it one night when taking Danny home
28   after a particularly raucous night at Chuggie's. Danny mentioned hearing it was a good route to
29   take if you wanted to avoid cops and were in a hurry. I told Danny that a lot of people used to
30   use Canyon to sneak home from the bars, but too many people had died on that road—speed-
31   ing and losing control, going too fast to see the road, swerving to avoid deer—so now there
32   were always cops patrolling the road at night. Danny said, "Thanks for the tip! I guess a cab is
33   a smarter bet," which was just what I wanted to hear.
34

35   It was pouring rain the night Vanessa died—there was actually a flash flood warning for the
36   lower lying areas in Nita Center due to the torrential rainfall, and it started pouring a little before
37   1:00 a.m., when the paper said the crash happened. If Danny was speeding on that stretch, given
38   the conditions, it's no surprise that the car ended up off the road and wrapped around a tree.
39

40   I feel awful for Vanessa Sullivan and her family—and for Danny and the other passenger as
41   well. I keep thinking I should have said something to Danny or maybe jumped out and taken
42   away the keys. But I didn't really think Danny was that bad off by the time Danny got behind
43   the wheel. I mean, Danny wasn't sober, but most of the people who leave that bar and get
44   behind the wheel have had a couple of drinks. I've been there myself—I mean, hasn't every-
45   body? Still, I know they'd have been fine if they had been in my cab.

1   Of the exhibits in this case, I am familiar with the following: Accident Photos 0010 through
2   0015, which were shown to me by attorneys in this case and which I agree are accurate depic-
3   tions of images contained therein of Canyon Road. I am also familiar with the Chuggie's Drink
4   Menu, and except where specifically noted in my affidavit, I have no reason to believe that any
5   of the drinks served on September 24 either omitted a component listed or added a component
6   not listed on the drink menu. I am not familiar with any other exhibits or affidavits other than
7   my own.

I hereby attest to having read the above statement and swear or affirm it to be my own. I also swear or affirm to the truthfulness of its content. Before giving this statement, I was told it should contain everything I knew that might be relevant to my testimony, and I followed those instructions. I also understand that I can and must update this affidavit if anything new occurs to me until the moment before I testify in this case.

_____/s/ SL_____
Sam Lyons

Subscribed and sworn before me on this, the 1st day of October, YR-2.

_____/s/ SS_____
Sarah Shelton, Notary Public

AFFIDAVIT OF ASHLEY NORTON

After being duly sworn upon oath, Ashley Norton hereby deposes and states as follows.

1   My name is Ashley Norton. I am a professor of medicine at Nita State University. I have a
2   bachelor's degree in chemistry from Brown University, and I earned my master's degree and
3   doctorate in forensic science from Johns Hopkins University in YR-17. As stated in my cur-
4   riculum vitae, I have particular expertise in alcohol testing and alcohol pharmacology.
5
6   I have testified in over 100 cases regarding the use of alcohol tests, most of which involved the
7   use of various models of the Intoxilyzer breath alcohol content analysis machine. In each of
8   those cases I testified for the defense. I have been hired by the defense in this case to provide
9   my expertise regarding breath alcohol and blood alcohol concentrations (BAC) and the use
10 of breath alcohol concentration (BrAC) analysis machines to determine such concentrations.
11 I have also been asked to analyze the evidence in this case regarding Danny Dawson's con-
12 sumption of alcohol and resulting breath and blood alcohol concentration on September 25,
13 YR-2. I am charging my standard rate of $250 per hour for my time and expertise. To date,
14 I have worked twenty hours on this case, for a total of $5,000 in expert fees. I will be paid an
15 additional flat fee of $2,000 if I am called to testify in court.
16
17 Law enforcement would like you to believe that the BrAC analysis machines they use are
18 infallible. They are not. Danny Dawson's attorneys came to me with the results of a BrAC test
19 given the night that Dawson was involved in an accident and wanted to know if there had been
20 any error. I sat down with Dawson to recreate the events of that night, including a timeline
21 of Dawson's drinking. Then I worked backwards, taking the BrAC that the police obtained
22 (which I got from the official analysis report) and tried to match it to the number of drinks that
23 Dawson told me Dawson had consumed. I'll walk you through that process.
24
25 In the early twentieth century, Dr. E.M.P. Widmark developed a formula to determine the
26 number of drinks an individual had consumed based on six variables. These variables were
27 1) the amount consumed, 2) the body weight, 3) the blood alcohol concentration (BAC), 4) the
28 alcohol elimination rate, 5) the time since the first drink, and 6) the fluid ounces of alcohol per
29 drink. At that time, the volume of distribution was assumed to be a constant, but we'll look at
30 that in a moment. Of course, this equation can be used to solve for any of the variables, assum-
31 ing that six are known.
32
33 Dr. Widmark later observed that this equation did not apply equally to men and women, so he
34 developed a confidence interval that took this variance into account, to the best of his ability
35 and the available science. Unfortunately, Dr. Widmark did not have all of the research that
36 we have today. His formula provides a good estimate, but with a margin of error that may be
37 several drinks wide.
38
39 Although modern science has evolved beyond Widmark's equation, we still use a similar
40 formula. Since we're trying to estimate Dawson's BAC at the time Dawson was driving,

1   we need to look at the equation a little differently than Widmark did. An individual's blood

2   alcohol concentration is now looked at as mostly dependent on five variables. These vari-

3   ables are 1) the total amount of alcohol consumed, 2) the rate of absorption, 3) the first-pass

4   metabolism amount, 4) the volume of distribution, and 5) the rate of ethanol elimination.

5   I will address each of these factors separately. The sixth variable that Widmark was concerned

6   with—time—applies as it does in the Widmark equation.

7

8   All else being equal, the amount of alcohol consumed will have the greatest effect on an indi-

9   vidual's peak BAC. The more that is consumed, the higher the BAC will rise. This is true across

10   genders, different body-mass indices, ages, and all other factors. However, exactly how high

11   the BAC will rise is dependent on those factors.

12

13   Beyond the total amount consumed, the rate of absorption matters. The rate will be faster if the

14   stomach is empty and is a function of the concentration of the alcohol consumed. A higher con-

15   centration of alcohol, such as a shot of liquor compared to a beer, causes a greater concentra-

16   tion gradient. This drives up the rate of absorption. However, if the concentrations are too high,

17   there may be slower gastric emptying of stomach contents into the small intestines. This affects

18   BAC because the small intestines provide quicker, more complete absorption of the alcohol.

19   Studies done on gastric emptying rates indicate that men will absorb more alcohol than women,

20   but this is not the only factor that impacts absorption, as I will explain.

21

22   Third, one must consider the first-pass metabolism. The rate of elimination of alcohol matters

23   significantly when drinks are consumed over an extended period of time. Before alcohol is

24   processed by the small intestines, it is first metabolized in the stomach by the enzyme alcohol

25   dehydrogenase ("ADH"). ADH, because it is found in the stomach, drives the primary process

26   for alcohol elimination. Although other enzymes are capable of doing this, studies show that

27   ADH is the most important enzyme in the body's processing of alcohol.

28

29   Studies that I am familiar with have demonstrated that women have less ADH than men do and

30   this causes them to have a lower first-pass metabolism. The lower the metabolism is, the greater

31   the absorption. This has implications for peak BAC that can make the gender of the individual

32   relevant when estimating the time a peak BAC occurred.

33

34   Things are complicated further by an individual's level of body water. The volume of distribu-

35   tion is based on the overall body water of an individual. This is where gender also affects peak

36   BAC. Typically, men have a greater water content in their body compared to women. This is

37   because muscle tissue has a higher water content than fatty tissue. Alcohol is largely distributed

38   into body water, which leads to lower BACs, drink-for-drink and pound-for-pound, in men

39   compared to women.

40

41   Without an understanding of each of these factors, one cannot estimate what a given individual's

42   peak BAC will be given a specific amount of alcohol consumed. When I interviewed Dawson

43   before I performed my analysis, Dawson told me that Dawson had approximately one drink per

44   hour that Dawson was at Chuggie's. These drinks included one beer and three mixed drinks from

45   2:00 p.m. to 6:00 p.m., and then a whiskey on the rocks, a shot, a beer, a whiskey-and-ginger-ale,

1 and a tequila sunrise between 6:30 p.m. and 12:30 a.m. Dawson told me that Dawson did not
2 drink any screwdrivers, although there were several on Dawson's bar tab. I did not corroborate
3 Dawson's story. I operated under the assumption that each drink contained the same amount of
4 alcohol found in a generally accepted shot, beer, or glass of wine. If the drinks that Dawson had
5 were stronger or weaker than those standards, then my findings would be different. *undermines*
6 *her point*
7 Dawson also told me that the drinks Dawson had were consumed evenly over a period of nine
8 and a half hours. Dawson also told me that Dawson ate a burger, coleslaw, and an extra-large
9 order of cheese fries with the first drink. My analysis takes all of Dawson's demographic and
10 physiological data (gender, age, weight, etc.) into consideration.
11
12 After reviewing all of these in relation to Dawson and the particulars of this case, I was able
13 to reach the conclusion that Dawson's BAC at the time of the accident was around 0.08.
14 Of course, my determination would change if it turned out that Dawson had more to drink
15 than Dawson told me or if the drinks were stronger than the standard drink (fourteen grams of
16 alcohol per drink). So if Dawson's true blood alcohol concentration was below the legal limit,
17 how could the police analysis be so far off? After all, the final measurement is over twice the
18 legal limit. There are several things that help explain this.
19
20 Most breath-testing devices will render a cumulative reading of all alcohols in the body
21 (ingested and auto-generated). This means that other alcohols, like isopropyl alcohol, will be
22 measured as if it was ethanol. Endogenous isopropyl alcohol is part of the physiological reac-
23 tion to the toxicity of acetone or ketone buildup. As the ketone level rises, the body uses certain
24 amino acids to create enzyme pathways, which remove or convert the ketones into safer com-
25 pounds. Isopropyl alcohol is one of those safer compounds. One pathway uses the enzyme
26 ADH. This is the same enzyme the liver uses to break down ethanol into acetaldehyde. Both
27 of these pathways can cause higher BrAC readings, even if the individual being tested has not
28 had a single drink. This is the same type of effect that persons with hypoglycemia, a condi-
29 tion involving low blood sugar levels, might experience. If Dawson had low blood sugar, the
30 results could be highly skewed, too. The food that Dawson ate was consumed around six hours
31 before the crash, plenty of time for digestion to occur and for Dawson's blood sugar to drop
32 again. The Intoxilyzer 8000, which was used in this case, does a fairly good job at screening
33 out substances that are not ethanol, but no machine is perfect.
34
35 The Intoxilyzer 8000, the model used by the Nita Department of Forensics for BrAC testing,
36 uses a set ratio of blood to air when calculating the BAC value for any individual. This allows
37 the machine to convert BrAC into BAC for the read-out, but this is where one major problem
38 with BrAC to BAC conversion lies. This ratio is 2100:1, or the same amount (weight) of alco-
39 hol will be found in 2.1 L of deep lung breath as will be found in 1 cc of pulmonary blood. The
40 problem with this ratio is that it varies markedly among individuals and even within a given
41 individual over time. Studies that are accepted and widely used in my field have routinely
42 demonstrated that the ratio is higher during the absorption phase and lower during the elimina-
43 tion phase. This means that an individual will blow a higher BrAC while they are eliminating
44 alcohol from their system than they would when they are absorbing it, even though the true
45 BAC should be the same.

1   It cannot be stressed more that the breath-to-blood ratio is perhaps the most important factor

2   in determining the validity of a BrAC result. All of the studies I have done, as well as those

3   studies done by other doctors around the United States, two studies in the United Kingdom, as

4   well a study in Japan that I participated in, demonstrate that an individual's true ratio can vary

5   from 900:1 all the way to 3400:1. This range has staggering implications for all breath alcohol

6   test machines. If Dawson had a true ratio on the lower end of that spectrum, then the BrAC

7   result obtained that night would need to be cut in half. If Dawson's true ratio were 1100:1, then

8   Dawson's true blood alcohol concentration would be 52.38 percent of the BrAC obtained. That

9   is 52.38 percent of 0.19, which is just below 0.1. Even so, if Dawson's ratio were lower, which

10   I very much doubt, Dawson would be over the legal limit.

11

12   There is also the temperature of Dawson's breath to consider. The Intoxilyzer 8000 uses a value

13   of $34.2° \pm .2$ C. A variation of just $1°$C can skew the results by as much as 10 percent by making

14   the alcohol more volatile and shifting the partition ratio further away from 2100:1. It should be

15   noted, however, that Dawson's BrAC measurement was high enough that temperature probably

16   played a negligible role, if indeed it played a role at all.

17

18   Lastly, however, the existence of mouth alcohol can skew a BrAC analysis. As any expert

19   trained in the administration of a breath alcohol test can tell you, the presence of alcohol in

20   the mouth during the sample collection phases can render any reading much higher than the

21   true reading should be. Mouth alcohol can come from a variety of sources. It may be trapped

22   in dental work, have come from mints or mouthwashes, be endogenous to the system (e.g., the

23   isopropyl alcohol I talked about earlier), or be the result of vomit, a belch, a burp, or even acid

24   reflux. Typically, the presence of mouth alcohol will cause the machine to spike before drop-

25   ping down and leveling out, which will result in an error message. Still, it is possible for suffi-

26   cient alcohol to be in the mouth that such a drop will not occur. If there is no drop, the machine

27   cannot tell the difference between breath alcohol and mouth alcohol.

28

29   I asked Dawson about all of these factors. Dawson said that Dawson had not had any dental

30   work done recently. Dawson confirmed that the arresting officer had asked Dawson if Dawson

31   had used mouthwash or mints; Dawson had not. When I asked, Dawson told me that Dawson

32   had not thrown up that night. I asked Dawson if the officer had told Dawson not to burp or belch

33   or if the officer had asked about acid reflux. Dawson seemed confused and said that the officer

34   had never mentioned that. I went back to look at the police report and at the BrAC printout, but

35   I could not find any evidence that Dawson was ever asked about it. I asked Dawson if Dawson

36   could remember burping or having acid reflux. Dawson said sure and told me that the burger

37   and cheese fries that Dawson ate had given Dawson some heartburn, but Dawson couldn't

38   remember if Dawson had burped or had any acid reflux after Dawson was arrested and before

39   the breath test.

40

41   Why could a little bit of acid reflux affect a BrAC reading so much? Well, the air sample taken

42   by an Intoxilyzer 8000 is only a couple of liters, and the calculations done by the machine

43   require that initial measurement to be multiplied by a factor of 100 in order to obtain a concen-

44   tration value of grams per 210 liters.

[handwritten margin note beside lines 31–34: "officer never told him not to burp"]

1   Now, am I saying that Dawson had a blood alcohol concentration of less than 0.08? Absolutely
2   not. It seems inarguable to me that Dawson was too intoxicated to drive. However, based on
3   the amount of alcohol that Dawson consumed, my calculations show that Dawson should
4   not have been anywhere near 0.19. I don't think Dawson is lying about the number of drinks
5   Dawson had, but I suspect the drinks were stronger than the amount we use to calculate blood
6   alcohol concentration (14 grams of alcohol per standard drink). Was Dawson intoxicated? Yes.
7   Was Dawson grossly intoxicated? No. Dawson may not even have felt much effect; one of the
8   symptoms of intoxication at that level is the underestimation of impairment. So why did the
9   Intoxilyzer show such a high reading? There are probably several factors. I would say that
10 the main problems with the BrAC reading that we have for Dawson that night have to do with
11 the partition ratio and the presence of mouth alcohol.
12
13 I have included all of my conclusions and all of the bases for those conclusions in this affidavit.
14 In coming to my conclusions, I reviewed the Intoxilyzer test results and spoke with Dawson
15 about Dawson's experience. When reaching my conclusions, I only relied on the documents
16 that I mention using in my affidavit. When it comes to blood alcohol levels and behavior,
17 I agree that the Benton and Carman treatise is the leading treatise and is entirely correct.
18
19 Of the available exhibits, I am familiar with the following: Bar Tab #1 of Danny Dawson,
20 Bar Tab #2 of Danny Dawson, and Bar Tab of Vanessa Sullivan; Intoxylizer 8000 Operator's
21 Checklist; BrAC testing form; BrAC results; the article "Alcohol Ingestion and the Human
22 Body," which I relied upon in reaching my conclusions in this case; and the Curriculum Vitae
23 of Ashley Norton, which I wrote myself. I am also familiar with the Chuggie's Drink Menu,
24 and except where specifically noted in my affidavit, I have no reason to believe that any of the
25 drinks served at Chuggie's on September 24 or 25, YR-2, either omitted a component listed on
26 the drink menu or added a component not listed on the drink menu. I am not familiar with any
27 of the other available exhibits or affidavits other than my own.

I hereby attest to having read the above statement and swear or affirm it to be my own. I also
swear or affirm to the truthfulness of its content. Before giving this statement, I was told it
should contain everything I knew that might be relevant to my testimony, and I followed those
instructions. I also understand that I can and must update this affidavit if anything new occurs
to me until the moment before I testify in this case.

_____/s AN_____
Dr. Ashley Norton

Subscribed and sworn before me on this, the 3rd day of October, YR-1.

_____/s SS_____
Sarah Shelton, Notary Public

AFFIDAVIT OF LESLIE ROMAN

After being duly sworn upon oath, Leslie Roman hereby deposes and states as follows.

1   My name is Leslie Roman. I own an accident-reconstruction firm located on Main Street in
2   Nita Center. The firm reviews and analyzes facts regarding an accident determines, to the
3   extent scientifically possible, what actually happened. I also help rural municipalities by
4   reviewing road-design proposals and road-safety questions from time to time. I don't do that
5   for the money, though. I just think it's important to have safe roads in our state. When it comes
6   to paying the bills, I do that by reconstructing accidents for private parties.
7

8   Most of my work for private parties is in the context of civil cases—I have testified in over thirty
9   civil cases—but I have also testified as an expert in seventeen criminal cases in Nita. In civil
10   cases, I'm equally likely to testify for the plaintiff or the defendant. In criminal cases, the state
11   always uses personnel from its Fatal Crash Team (FCT), so I testify only for the defense if I am
12   called. In a large number of criminal cases, I've had to turn down clients because I've found
13   no issues at all with the FCT's work. As is common, my work has regularly been reviewed by
14   other experts in the field. I have never received a negative review. I have been accepted as an
15   expert on accident reconstruction in court every time I have been called to testify.
16

17   My involvement with Danny Dawson's case started on October 14, YR-2, when I was con-
18   tacted by counsel for the defendant to look into the case. I was warned before I started that
19   the victim of the crash was the daughter of the district attorney, Ms. Sullivan, and that counsel
20   understood if I wanted to stay away from the case. This was all the more reason for me to take
21   a look into this accident. I wanted to make sure that the government was not blinded by the
22   need to blame. I took on the case for my standard hourly rate of $200 per hour, which was
23   to be paid regardless of the conclusions I reached. I should note that if I testify at trial, then
24   I will be paid an additional flat fee of $2,000 on top of the $5,000 I have already been paid for
25   compiling my expert report.
26

27   All of my conclusions are detailed in my report, which I provided to both parties in advance of
28   trial. The basis of analysis listed in my expert report is a complete list of all of the information
29   I relied upon in drawing conclusions. Before trial, I was granted access to all of the statements,
30   affidavits, and exhibits that defense counsel told me could be relevant to my work in this case.
31   Reading through all of these documents did not change any of my conclusions, nor does any
32   of the additional evidence permit me to draw any new conclusions not already stated in my
33   report and/or affidavit. The information included in the statements I reviewed is identical to the
34   relevant information in the affidavits prepared for this case.
35

36   My work in this case was limited to accident reconstruction. While I am aware of statements
37   from various individuals regarding Danny Dawson's having consumed alcohol the night of
38   the accident, I am neither qualified nor able to give any opinion whatsoever on Dawson's
39   actual level of sobriety on the night of the crash or on the validity or reliability of any tests
40   used to evaluate sobriety performed by the Nita Center Police Department. I am also in no

1   position, based on the evidence available, to determine conclusively whether a deer ran in front

2   of Dawson's car immediately prior to the accident, as Dawson states. I can state, however, that

3   Dawson's operation of the vehicle in the moments leading up to the accident was consistent

4   with those of a driver swerving to avoid a suddenly appearing obstacle (such as a deer) and then

5   overcorrecting in an attempt to regain control of the vehicle and get back on the road. Dawson

6   could have gone off the right side of the road for any number of other reasons. I focused on

7   the theory that a deer jumped out in the road because I was specifically asked to evaluate the

8   plausibility of Dawson's account of the accident.

9

10   I understand that I reached a different conclusion about the speed at which Dawson was travel-

11   ing when Dawson ran off the road than the FCT member on the scene, Officer Ryan Foster. It's

12   clearly an advantage for Foster that Foster was on the scene on the day of the crash. However,

13   Foster's calculations appear to overestimate the speed of the vehicle prior to the accident, as

14   stated in my expert report. I wholeheartedly agree with Foster that the primer by Windsor

15   and Strasberg, "Vehicle Accident Reconstruction," is the most relied-upon and reliable treatise

16   in the field. My calculations and conclusions regarding the vehicle's speed are completely

17   explained by the Windsor and Strasberg primer, and I relied on no other method of calculation

18   in making them.

19

20   I also think that Foster understates the dangers of Canyon Road in the FCT report. The road was

21   so dangerous at the spot of the accident that a guardrail was erected right where the accident

22   occurred extraordinarily soon after the accident. It's pretty clear to me that there always should

23   have been a guardrail. Having trees so close to a curve on a dangerous road with wildlife often

24   in the area, no guardrail, and a narrow shoulder is simply not acceptable. I have to believe that

25   Vanessa Sullivan would still be alive if there was a guardrail on the side of Canyon Road that

26   kept her side of the car from ever slamming into a tree. I guess something terrible could have

27   happened even with a guardrail, but I'm not so sure about that.

28

29   When I worked for the Nita Department of Transportation, I actually compiled a report of

30   danger spots on roads that needed fixing at the direction of my supervisor, Chet Vardy. I am

31   almost certain that this exact curve on Canyon Road was part of the report. It's sad to think

32   that Nita did nothing for a decade about that problem and that it took the death of a prominent

33   prosecutor's child to bring about change.

34

35   I should mention that I worked for Vanessa Sullivan's father at Global Motors Manufactur-

36   ing Center. While I was working there, I told him about some kids that put toilet paper on

37   my house and threw eggs at it and that I was trying to decide whether I should press charges.

38   He told me that his wife, a young prosecutor at the time, got some kids convicted of felonies

39   when they did that to the Sullivan home. I thought that was pretty extreme. Ever since that

40   day, I've been concerned about the severity of punishment in cases where the prosecutor's

41   office is even tangentially involved. It doesn't quite seem right to me. Come to think of it, this

42   is only the third time I have ever testified in a trial in Nita where the defendant was charged

43   with murder for drunk driving, and all three of them involved victims with close ties to the

44   prosecutor's office.

[Handwritten margin note, left: "she would still be alive"]

[Handwritten note, bottom: "→ pattern of overly harsh punishment for things impacting prosecutor's office"]

1   Of the affidavits and exhibits in this case, I am familiar with the following and only the
2   following: Curriculum Vitae of Leslie Roman, Expert Report of Leslie Roman, Expert Report
3   of Leslie Roman—Crime Scene Diagram, and Accident Photos 0008 through 0015, all of
4   which I created; the article "Vehicle Accident Reconstruction: A Primer," which I relied upon
5   in reaching my conclusions; Voicemail Message, Nita FCT Officer Report, FCT Diagram, and
6   Accident Photos 0001 through 0007, all of which I received from the police; the affidavits of
7   London Bennett and Taylor Hopson, which I was provided by counsel; and my own affidavit.

I hereby attest to having read the above statement and swear or affirm it to be my own. I also swear or affirm to the truthfulness of its content. Before giving this statement, I was told it should contain everything I knew that might be relevant to my testimony, and I followed those instructions. I also understand that I can and must update this affidavit if anything new occurs to me until the moment before I testify in this case.

_____/s/ LR_____
Leslie Roman

Subscribed and sworn before me on this, the 1st day of October, YR-1.

_____/s/ SS_____
Sarah Shelton, Notary Public

AFFIDAVIT OF AVERY SMITH

After being duly sworn upon oath, Dr. Avery Smith hereby deposes and states as follows.

1   My name is Avery Smith, and I am the Director of the Nita Department of Forensic Science.
2   I work out of our main lab at the Nita Center Police Department Headquarters. In addition to
3   directing the department, I also provide research and scientific support for Nita's breath alcohol
4   testing program. When the need arises, I also provide interpretation of blood and breath alcohol
5   results and testify as an expert on the subject. It is in that capacity that I offer my expertise today.
6

7   There are several options for law enforcement when performing alcohol level tests on indi-
8   viduals suspected of driving under the influence. The most common, and most widely used,
9   testing method is breath alcohol concentration (BrAC). Here in Nita we use the Intoxilyzer
10   8000, which is used in dozens of other states. The Intoxilyzer 8000 is listed on the National
11   Highway Traffic Safety Administration's Conforming Products List as an approved device and
12   is an industry standard.
13

14   The Intoxilyzer 8000 is a device that collects a series of sample breaths that are then passed
15   through a beam of infrared light. The amount of alcohol in the sample is measured based upon
16   the amount of light absorbed. It is more reliable than preliminary breath tests (also known as
17   PBTs, or non-evidential test devices) that offer law enforcement a baseline reading in the field.
18   These PBT devices are handheld and provide a BrAC reading, but the result is not admissible
19   in court. That's why officers must bring those who are suspected of driving under the influence
20   in for testing on an Intoxilyzer 8000 after they fail field sobriety tests or give a high reading
21   on a PBT.
22

23   The Intoxilyzer 8000 uses a set ratio of blood to air when calculating the blood alcohol con-
24   centration (BAC) value for any individual. This ratio is 2100:1, meaning that the same amount
25   (weight) of alcohol will be found in 2.1 L of deep lung breath as will be found in 1 cc of pulmo-
26   nary blood. In this way, the BrAC can be converted into BAC, which is the standard measure-
27   ment used for DUI under Nita state law. This conversion method has been widely accepted in
28   the scientific and law enforcement communities, and it is relied upon by many states, including
29   Nita, as an accurate method of determining BAC from a properly administered breath alcohol
30   test on approved equipment.
31

32   Shortly before 1:00 a.m. on September 25, Officer Ryan Foster called me at the station.
33   According to Foster, the defendant had been driving a YR-3 Chevrolet Impala when the car
34   veered off the road and into a tree, causing one fatality. The officer suspected that the defen-
35   dant had been drinking and performed three field sobriety tests, as per Nita Police Procedure.
36   When the defendant failed all three of the field sobriety tests, the police officer that performed
37   those tests on the scene brought Dawson to the station.
38

39   Before Foster arrived with Dawson, we got a call from Ryan Sullivan, the District Attorney in
40   Nita Center. Captain Morrison and I took the call on speakerphone. Sullivan was distraught

be careful running tests

1   and told us that her daughter was dead and that I would need to run an Intoxilyzer test on a
2   DUI suspect involved in the crash. Sullivan reminded me to be careful running the tests, though
3   I didn't need any reminding, especially under the circumstances. I had been calibrating one of
4   our Intoxilyzer 8000s, which are evidential test devices, just before Sullivan's call in response
5   to Foster's earlier heads-up. I went back and finished the calibration while Foster watched
6   Dawson in the holding cell.
7
8   As soon as I was finished calibrating the Intoxilyzer, I gave Dawson a BrAC test using the
9   device. In Nita, we follow a standard procedure when using the Intoxilyzer 8000. Here at the
10 Department of Forensics, we provide equipment, trainings, supplies, and lab support for all lev-
11 els of law enforcement in the state. As the director, I am personally responsible for establishing
12 the operating procedures for all of our breath-testing devices, including the Intoxilyzer 8000.
13 Only testers who have been trained and certified by my department have the authority to con-
14 duct breath tests. When conducting a breath test using the Intoxilyzer 8000, all certified opera-
15 tors are required to follow and fill out the Intoxilyzer 8000 operator's checklist. This ensures
16 that the machine is used properly. I am a certified operator.
17
18 The Intoxilyzer 8000 has many different parts that the operator must be aware. The first is the
19 mouthpiece that must be used. Made out of plastic, this trap is designed to keep debris and
20 excess moisture out of the machine. Excess moisture—for example, saliva or vomit—can cause
21 the machine to register an elevated reading. The mouthpiece connects to a heated breath tube,
22 where the sample is collected before being analyzed by the machine. There is also a simulator
23 (i.e., a control) sample, which is used to ensure that the machine is working properly. The simu-
24 lator sample, which should yield a BrAC of 0.08, is kept at a constant temperature, keeping the
25 air-to-alcohol ratio constant. The machine is designed to tolerate temperature differences of up
26 to 0.2 degrees Celsius, or a range of 33.8 to 34.2. This is because human breath is calculated
27 at 34 degrees Celsius.
28
29 At the beginning of every test, the machine runs several blanks and simulator samples to estab-
30 lish an accuracy level and a precision level. If any of those tests are out of the expected range,
31 the machine will return an "OUT OF TOLERANCE" error message, and the operator must
32 contact the Department of Forensics for diagnostic assistance and troubleshooting. Often such
33 an error message indicates a problem with the simulator solution, not with the machine itself.
34
35 On the night that I tested Danny Dawson, I had just changed out the simulator solution, and
36 I did not receive an error message when I started running the machine. The simulator read-
37 ings were accurate, giving the expected BrAC value of 0.08, and the temperature sensors were
38 in range.
39
40 Before I took Dawson back for the Intoxilyzer test, I asked the police officer who brought
41 Dawson to the station, Officer Foster, whether or not Dawson had been observed for the previ-
42 ous fifteen minutes. The testing procedures require a subject to be observed for at least fifteen
43 minutes before any test. This part of the procedure is used to ensure that no residual mouth
44 alcohol is present. Mouth alcohol can cause a much higher BrAC reading than would represent
45 the amount of alcohol actually in that person's body. There can be several causes of mouth

1   alcohol. The usual suspects are mouthwash, certain types of mints, very recent consumption
2   of alcohol, a gastric event (such as vomiting or eructation, also know as burping or belching),
3   and acid reflux. The observation period is meant to allow whatever alcohol could be deposited
4   in the mouth time to evaporate.
5
6   The officer said that Dawson had been cuffed at the scene and that the ride to the station had
7   been approximately ten minutes long, and that Foster had been standing outside Dawson's cell
8   for approximately ten minutes since Dawson was put in the cell. Since mouth alcohol dissi-
9   pates well within the standard fifteen-minute window of required observation, there is no way
10 that Dawson still had mouth alcohol present as a result of drinking at the bar. I checked with
11 the officer to make sure that Dawson did not have access to alcohol, breath mints, or mouth-
12 wash during that time. The officer also said that Dawson did not appear to vomit or burp, but
13 I don't remember if I asked Dawson whether or not this was true. Typically, you don't want
14 to let a suspect know that burping may throw off the machine because the person might start
15 burping on purpose, which makes it impossible to run a test. Whenever possible, I spend
16 fifteen minutes talking to the suspect, just to be absolutely sure that they don't burp or belch
17 prior to the test.
18
19 I did spend a couple of minutes talking to Dawson while I set up the machine, and Dawson
20 slurred words, spoke loudly, and indicated a moderate level of intoxication. Dawson told me
21 that I was wasting my time and didn't seem happy to have to be tested, but would you be
22 happy? Dawson was ultimately cooperative. Dawson never appeared to burp or belch. Because
23 the officer told me that Dawson had been observed for nearly twenty minutes between the car
24 ride and the holding cell, I only waited five minutes before starting the test. I've observed
25 hundreds of individuals during Intoxilyzer tests, and, based on my experience and Dawson's
26 behavior, I estimated that Dawson's breath alcohol would be around the legal limit.
27
28 The variable testing phase, using Dawson's breath, was run on two samples to ensure preci-
29 sion, as required by the standard protocol. The readings must be within 0.02 of each other for
30 the breath test to count. I had Dawson provide two samples using the mouthpiece I described
31 before. Dawson's readouts were 0.194 and 0.191. The machine compares the two samples,
32 takes the lower of the two, and truncates the reading to two digits for the final result, so
33 Dawson's official reading was 0.19.
34
35 I believe that these test results are accurate, though I was surprised that both of them were well
36 over the Nita state legal limit of 0.08. Dawson's results can't be blamed on other factors, such
37 as the mouth alcohol as mentioned above. If there was any residual alcohol left in Dawson's
38 mouth, the machine would have picked it up. Mouth alcohol will generally cause a spike in the
39 BrAC curve detected by the unit, followed by a marked decrease as the air from the lungs is
40 expelled. There was no such spike in Dawson's test.
41
42 Using rough estimates that apply generally, we can estimate the number of drinks that Dawson
43 consumed. The average person can process one drink per hour (fourteen grams of alcohol) and
44 stay under the legal limit. Dawson told me that Dawson had approximately one drink per hour
45 while Dawson was at the bar. If that's true, I don't know how Dawson's BrAC was still at 0.19

1   at two in the morning, which is when I tested Dawson. <u>Either Dawson had more drinks than</u>

2   <u>that and lied to me, or Dawson processes alcohol much slower than the average person</u> used to

3   calculate that rate. I never got a chance to examine Dawson as a physician, so I can't tell you

4   Dawson's weight or family background, both of which are integral to determining how many

5   drinks a person may have had given a certain BrAC. Just looking at someone isn't enough to

6   estimate those factors, so even if I saw Dawson again today, I wouldn't be able to give a better

7   opinion than that, unless I were allowed to have a medical doctor examine Dawson and obtain

8   a medical history.

9

10   All of my conclusions and the bases for those conclusions are included in this affidavit.

11   In reaching conclusions, I relied on the Intoxilyzer 8000 test results and my personal observa-

12   tions and training. Since I conducted the test myself, I completed all of the paperwork related

13   to the testing, such as the standard operational checklist. I can also vouch for the fact that the

14   Benton and Carman treatise on intoxication is the leader in the field and is completely accurate.

15

16   Of the available exhibits, I am familiar with the following and only the following: NHTSA

17   list of approved BrAC units; Intoxilyzer 8000 Operator's Checklist; BrAC testing form; BrAC

18   results; the article "Alcohol Ingestion and the Human Body," which I relied on in coming to my

19   conclusions in this case; and "Curriculum Vitae of Avery Smith," which I wrote myself. I am

20   also familiar with the Chuggie's Drink Menu, and unless specifically noted elsewhere in my

21   affidavit, I have no reason to believe that any of the drinks served on September 24 or 25, YR-2,

22   either omitted a component listed on the drink menu or added a component not listed on the

23   drink menu. I am not familiar with any other available exhibits or affidavits other than my own.

I hereby attest to having read the above statement and swear or affirm it to be my own. I also swear or affirm to the truthfulness of its content. Before giving this statement, I was told it should contain everything I knew that might be relevant to my testimony, and I followed those instructions. I also understand that I can and must update this affidavit if anything new occurs to me until the moment before I testify in this case.

_____
/s/ AS
Dr. Avery Smith

Subscribed and sworn before me on this, the 3rd day of October, YR-1.

_____
/s/ SS
Sarah Shelton, Notary Public

[Handwritten margin note beside lines 1–6: "don't examine him to get him to get vital info on alc absorp"]

AFFIDAVIT OF SANDY CULLEN

After being duly sworn upon oath, Sandy Cullen hereby deposes and states as follows.

1   I just want to start this out by being perfectly clear. I'm not one of those crazy Occupy protest-
2   ers. I'm not even *related* to one of those Occupy protestors, so none of this should have ever
3   happened in the first place. I might as well begin at the beginning. I live in Nita Center, Nita.
4   Right by the courthouse, about two streets over on Willow Street, there is a row of brown-
5   stones converted into apartments—rather nice, if I do say so myself. I own them, and I lease
6   them out; that's how I make my living. I live in the last building, a pretty blue unconverted
7   original, with my two dogs, Robie and Grace. But back to the Occupy bit of this story, because
8   that's the only reason I'm here in a room full of lawyers talking about something that never
9   should have happened in the first place.
10
11   It was September 24, YR-2. I had a busy day dealing with a complaint from the tenants in
12   Unit 3. At about six that evening, I met a friend of mine, a public defender, for dinner across
13   town at a beautiful little bistro called the Nita Inn. When we finished up around 8:30 p.m., we
14   decided to walk back through the town center and have a drink or two at the Courthouse Pub.
15
16   As we were walking back to the pub, we heard some scuffling in front of the courthouse. Some
17   police officers were giving three young people in bandanas a hard time. All three kids had
18   signs with those slogans from Occupy Nita on them. The national media never reported that
19   the Occupy protests started here a year before the hipsters in New York City stole the idea.
20   Anyway, I noticed a few other kids hanging around and a couple of tents. I looked over at my
21   friend and said, "Well, as long as they're not too loud, what's the harm?" My friend looked a
22   little more concerned. Then my friend reminded me that the protesters had been getting more
23   and more aggressive lately and that the police were just itching to arrest someone. I rolled my
24   eyes, and we walked around them to get to the Courthouse Pub.
25
26   I suppose we left around midnight. I only had two glasses of merlot, and I would have left
27   sooner, but a property lawyer cornered me, and we started talking about property values in
28   Nita Center and the state of my leases.
29
30   My friend called a cab, and I decided to walk home. I only live three blocks from the pub, after
31   all. The last thing my friend said to me was something about steering clear of the Occupy pro-
32   testors. I laughed and said that I would be fine. Looking back, I suppose I shouldn't have been
33   so cavalier about the whole thing, but I decided to cut across the steps of the courthouse. It's
34   the quickest way back to my brownstone, and it had begun to rain. I had forgotten my umbrella
35   at the bistro. It was dark, even with the lights in the green in front of the steps, and I tripped
36   over something on the ground. When I leaned down to see what it was, I noticed that it was
37   an empty forty of malt liquor. I looked around quickly to see if a protestor had dropped it, but
38   at that moment, they all seemed to have gone into their tents. I wasn't just going to leave the
39   bottle there! That's littering, and it's my neighborhood. There were some trash and recycling
40   receptacles at the end of the courthouse, so I bent down and picked up the bottle.

woah
aggressive
called DA
to "crack
protest"

1   Suddenly I was tackled from behind! All of a sudden there were floodlights and police every-
2   where. I felt a little dazed and confused. The cop who had taken me down was now holding the
3   bottle up and telling the others that I'd been drinking in public. Another one pulled me up and
4   peered into my eyes. She asked me if I was associated with the protestors. When I just looked
5   at her, because that was ridiculous, she asked me where I lived. I told her I lived here. I meant
6   in Nita Center, but that's not how she seemed to take it. "We got a live one!" she yelled, turning
7   me around and cuffing me. "Have you been drinking?" I told her I had been, but it had been
8   much earlier. "This one's been drinking!" she yelled. "Take 'em to the station," someone else
9   said. As I was shoved into the patrol car parked on the street, I heard her yell for someone to
10   call the district attorney—something about having finally cracked the protest.
11
12   I could feel a bruise where I'd been tackled. By the time they processed me in the station,
13   I knew that no one was going to listen to me. It was probably about 12:45 a.m. on Saturday by
14   the time they let me make my phone call. I called the friend I'd just gone to dinner with. "Don't
15   worry about it, Sandy, they're just hoping they've got a protestor."
16
17   "But I'm not!" I protested.
18
19   "I know that. You said they arrested you for drinking in public and being drunk in public? Don't
20   worry about that. I'll be there in forty minutes. Sit tight and don't say a word. Got it?"
21
22   I gritted my teeth and nodded.
23
24   "Sandy, you still there? Did you hear me?"
25
26   "Oh yeah, just practicing not saying a word."
27
28   Just then a police officer came over and told me to come with him—something about going in
29   the "drunk tank." He led me to a small cell near the front of the station. The cell was cinder-
30   block and had metal bars and two beds. "Try not to sober up," he said. "We still have to run a
31   breath test." Then he locked the door.
32
33   I was close enough to the front of the station that I could hear what the officers were talking
34   about—the usual, apparently, doughnuts and bad coffee. It was like I was stuck in a bad 1970s
35   police drama. A couple of phone calls came in, nothing too exciting, until all of a sudden the
36   woman who seemed to be in charge started barking orders and the phone wouldn't stop ringing.
37   Suddenly someone else was running down the hall from the other end of the station. I heard the
38   head cop call the person "Dr. Smith."
39
40   When Dr. Smith got there, the woman pressed the speakerphone button. I pressed my face
41   against the bars so that I could hear every word. "It's the DA," the head cop whispered to
42   Dr. Smith. "It sounds bad." Dr. Smith and the head officer both looked pretty nervous. That's
43   when the yelling started. At first I thought someone else had walked into the station, but then
44   I realized that it was a woman's voice over the phone, and boy, was she angry. I couldn't forget
45   what she said if I tried.

1   "Dr. Smith? Captain Morrison? It's Ryan Sullivan. Vanessa's—my daughter is dead." The DA
2   was clearly choked up. Smith gasped, and Morrison (the head cop) shook her head. The voice
3   on the phone continued, "On Canyon Road. It was a drunk driver named Danny Dawson.
4   Foster's doing the field sobriety tests now, and then Foster will send Dawson down to you for
5   a breath test." Then the voice on the phone turned icy. "Avery, you have to run the breath test.
6   I don't care how this has to go down, but Dawson is going away for murder. Do you under-
7   stand?" Smith looked at Morrison, and Morrison at Smith. "You hear me, Avery? Dawson
8   can't get away with this!"
9
10   Her voice became muffled, but if anything, the volume increased. She said some things
11   I couldn't understand and then shouted, "I'm going to make Dawson's life a living hell!"
12   I missed the rest of what she said. I didn't know if she was shouting at Dr. Smith and Captain
13   Morrison, or if she was yelling at someone on the other end, but I started getting worried
14   for Dawson, whoever Dawson was. But I guess that's what happens when you kill the DA's
15   daughter. Then the DA continued. "Avery, I don't need you messing up another test. There
16   needs to be no doubt that Dawson was way over the limit." At this point Morrison looked back
17   and saw me with my face pressed against the bars. She looked worried and grabbed the phone
18   off of the cradle and took it off of speakerphone. Dr. Smith told Captain Morrison that there
19   wouldn't be any problem. I didn't hear anything else. Dr. Smith went back to the other end
20   of the station.
21
22   After that phone call, I wasn't too surprised when a very wet-looking cop, who was introduced
23   to Captain Morrison as Officer Foster, dragged in a very nervous-looking, equally drenched
24   person that Officer Foster introduced as Danny Dawson. Foster dumped Dawson roughly on
25   a bench in the lobby of the station. Captain Morrison barked orders at a younger officer who
26   had been hanging around in the front of the office, and they approached Dawson. I overheard
27   Foster tell Morrison that Dawson failed every sobriety test in the field, but that Foster wasn't
28   sure how far over the limit Dawson actually was.
29
30   The younger officer grabbed at Dawson and said, "Get up, Dawson! You made a big mistake
31   killing the DA's daughter. You're coming with me." The officer led Dawson toward the back
32   of the station, with Foster alongside. The first thing I noticed about Dawson was that Dawson
33   couldn't seem to walk in a straight line. I mean here Dawson is, supported on either side by a
34   police officer, and Dawson is just dragging them all over the station. Dawson was yelling, "Get
35   off me! Get off me!" even though the officer was just trying to hold Dawson up. More than
36   once, they had to stop and let Dawson crouch down. Dawson was a mess. I thought Dawson
37   might throw up, but Dawson would stand back up and keep wobbling toward the cellblock.
38   I got the impression that the officers really wanted Dawson in a cell of Dawson's own, but it
39   took so long to just get to the cell I was in that one of them said, "It doesn't matter. This one
40   will be fine. Two drunks together won't make a bit of difference." I started to protest that gross
41   mischaracterization of me, when I remembered my friend's advice to say nothing until she got
42   there. Given that they'd taken my watch, I didn't know how long I still had to wait.
43
44   Officer Foster stood outside the cell watching Dawson and me for most of the time we were
45   there. It was kind of creepy. I don't even think Dawson knew Foster was there. Dawson looked

1   pretty bad off, so I got out of the way and let Dawson take the bottom bunk, Dawson said thanks
2   and said very loudly—almost yelling— "I'm Danny Dawson, who are you?" I answered, then
3   Dawson laid down, eyes closed. I waited about five seconds before my curiosity got the better
4   of me. I sat down next to Dawson on the bottom bunk and started to ask Dawson questions.
5   Dawson must have fallen asleep or had no idea where we were, because Dawson sat up quickly,
6   and Dawson's head smacked into the top bunk. Dawson looked at me like I'd come from outer
7   space and didn't seem to notice the head bump. Then Dawson asked me how I'd gotten into the
8   cell. When I told Dawson that I'd been in it when Dawson got there, Dawson looked confused
9   and laid back again, eyes closed.
10
11   I figured that Dawson was just plain drunk. I asked Dawson what had happened. Dawson said
12   there had been a car crash and it was complicated. I told Dawson about my day. Dawson sat up
13   and seemed pretty sympathetic. Dawson said I wasn't the only one getting railroaded. I nod-
14   ded and told Dawson to talk quietly, since I knew Foster was lurking outside. I mean, I haven't
15   passed the bar, but I know a little bit. Anyway, I told Dawson to start at the beginning.
16
17   "I had an interview, and it didn't go so well, so I went to the bar early. I met some friends for
18   dinner, and we stayed for a show. It wasn't even like I had that much to drink, maybe a drink
19   an hour. I can't quite remember now." Dawson was quiet, but was kind of slurring words.
20   If Dawson had only had a drink an hour, then Dawson must be a pretty cheap date. The younger
21   officer came back in a hurry—it couldn't have been more than two or three minutes. "Dawson!
22   Get up! You either have to take a breath test or sign a waiver saying you won't." The offi-
23   cer grabbed Dawson pretty roughly, given that Dawson wasn't giving him any trouble at all.
24   It seems to me that DA was already trying to make Dawson's life hell, Dawson's fault or not.
25
26   Dawson was brought back to the cell about fifteen minutes later and went straight back to lying
27   on the bunk. I was still pretty curious about the whole thing, so I asked Dawson if Dawson
28   had taken the Intoxilyzer test. "Doesn't matter, does it?" Dawson replied. "Mrs. Sullivan will
29   find some way to take me down whether she has that number or not." I started feeling bad
30   for Dawson.
31
32   One thing I had noticed about Dawson was that Dawson kept holding Dawson's head. At first
33   I thought that was because Dawson felt guilty, but then it started looking more like Dawson
34   was in pain, so I asked Dawson if Dawson was hurt. Dawson said that it didn't matter. I asked
35   Dawson again. "Yeah, my head hurts," Dawson finally admitted. "No one would look at me at
36   the scene. All they wanted to do was make me do tests, and Mrs. Sullivan was yelling . . . . I'll
37   be OK. I just have this horrible headache." I pointed out that Dawson had hit Dawson's head on
38   the bunk about twenty minutes before, and Dawson said, "I did?" Dawson flopped face down
39   on the bed, and I let Dawson lie quietly after that for a bit.
40
41   Well, I felt pretty bad for Dawson. It sure did sound like everyone was treating Dawson pretty
42   poorly. Then Dawson asked me, "Have you ever driven drunk?" I thought about it for a minute
43   and said no—well, not "*drunk* drunk," anyway. Dawson kept talking and said, "I mean, I've
44   driven when I've had more to drink than this. It was probably that stupid last shot—wasn't
45   even my fault. I'll bet it wasn't water. Who knows?" I realized that Dawson was talking to no

1   one in particular and just seemed to be saying things out loud. Then Dawson looked back at
2   me. "Do you think I was drunk?" Dawson asked. Dawson continued without my prompting,
3   "I was tipsy, maybe." I noticed that Dawson wasn't slurring as much as Dawson had been.
4   Dawson continued, "I never meant for anyone to get hurt. I hope Taylor and Vanessa are OK.
5   I just wanted us all to get home." I didn't have the heart to tell Dawson that Vanessa was dead.
6
7   I was about to tell Dawson that things would be OK when the young officer came back and
8   told me that my lawyer had called and he had to let me go. The officer looked really disap-
9   pointed about letting me go, too, but I didn't say anything smart to him after seeing how they
10 treated Dawson. As I left, Captain Morrison told me that I wasn't being charged with anything
11 because she had bigger fish to fry. I wonder just how they plan on frying Dawson, since it's
12 clear that that's what's going to happen.

I hereby attest to having read the above statement and swear or affirm it to be my own. I also swear or affirm to the truthfulness of its content. Before giving this statement, I was told it should contain everything I knew that might be relevant to my testimony, and I followed those instructions. I also understand that I can and must update this affidavit if anything new occurs to me until the moment before I testify in this case.

_____/s/ SEC_____
Sandy E. Cullen

Subscribed and sworn before me on this, the 3rd day of October, YR-1.

_____/s/ SS_____
Sarah Shelton, Notary Public